Table of Contents

The 5th Wave — By Rich Tennant

"Oh look, the hamsters are grooming again."

Hamsters
FOR
DUMMIES®

by Sarah Montague

WILEY

Wiley Publishing, Inc.

Hamsters For Dummies®

Published by
Wiley Publishing, Inc.
111 River St.
Hoboken, NJ 07030-5774
www.wiley.com

10 9 8 7 6

1B/RV/QT/QX/IN

Publisher's Acknowledgements

Project Editor: Joan Friedman
Acquisitions Editor: Stacy Kennedy
Technical Editor: Michael Callaghan
Composition Services: Indianapolis Composition Services Department
Cover Photo: © COK/Vikki Hart/Getty Images
Cartoon: Rich Tennant, www.the5thwave.com

About the Author

Sarah Montague is a writer and producer for print and public radio. She has covered the Westminster Kennel Club dog show for WNYC and National Public Radio for the past four years and has written for such publica-tions as *Animal Times* and *Eventing*. She is the coauthor of *The Complete Idiot's Guide to Horses* and the author of the forthcoming (from M. Evans) *Riding in Primetime*. She has also contributed cultural and animal-related features to nationally distributed programs such as *Morning Edition, On the Media,* and *Studio 360.* She lives with a cozy menagerie of dogs, cats, and rodents in upstate New York.

Dedication

To The Cowgirl Hall of Fame, where much of this book was written in good company, and to Emily and Charlotte, who taught me that big hearts come in small packages.

Chapter 1

Hankering for a Hamster

. . . .

In This Chapter

▶ Getting acquainted

▶ Tracing the hamster's path to domesticity

▶ Meeting the species of pet hamsters

▶ Examining hamster anatomy

. . . .

The old comic line "What's not to like?" fits hamsters perfectly. With their bright, inquisitive faces, agile bodies, and deft little paws, they've been engaging and entertaining families for generations.

Your decision to purchase a hamster may have been prompted by memories of a childhood friend. But whether this is your first hamster or just the first one you've had since you earned your allowance by cleaning the cage, you'll want to know how to make life safe and fun for your new companion, for yourself, and for your family.

How to Use This Book

Hamsters are hoarders, who stuff their cheek pouches full of goodies they may want to eat later. Think of this book the same way: as your secret cache of knowledge that you can use a little at a time, or all at once. You may have picked up this book along with your new hamster at the pet shop, or maybe you decided to read up on these animals before making a purchase. No matter where you started, this book tells you where to go next.

If you're interested in the history of the breed, I've included some tidbits of *olde* hamster for you to enjoy, but if you want to cut to the chase, I've made that easy too. The book is clearly organized in chapters you can read consecutively, or from which you can pick and choose to find out just want you need to know, just when you need to know it. Text in sidebars (the occasional gray box) is interesting but not essential, so you can skip them if you're in a hurry.

While reading *Hamsters For Dummies,* be on the lookout for these icons:

Paragraphs with this icon attached offer some juicy advice for making the most of your hamster experience.

When you see this icon, pay attention: The info in these paragraphs is worth storing in your mental filing cabinet.

This icon alerts you to information that helps you be the best pet owner possible by recognizing and avoiding potential dangers.

Paragraphs accompanied by this icon often contain medical or historical information and are not absolutely essential (unless you're earning a PhD in hamster).

While one breed of hamster, the Syrian Gold, is probably the most popular, in this book I also tell you about four other breeds that are common household pets, and what's fun and interesting about each.

Unfortunately, not all pet shops have knowledgeable staff, so use the pictures and descriptions in this book to help you determine what you've bought or are buying. Each breed of hamster differs, not only in size but also in temperament and some habits. The more you know, the more successful your hamster experience will be.

I explain what hamsters like to eat, how they socialize, what to look for in a healthy hamster, and how to spot the signs that yours may not be feeling too well. And because hamsters are very often pets in a family, I also talk about how to help your children love and care for their new friend, too.

Hate textbooks? Don't worry, this isn't one. Think of it as a picnic. Eat/read what you like, and put the rest back in the basket.

What Is a Hamster?

Hamsters, along with their kissing cousins the guinea pig, the vole, mice, and rats, are rodents. They have lots of company: About 40 percent of the world's mammal population is rodents — about 1,500 species out of some 4,000. (No wonder it's crowded out there!) House mice and lab rats may come to mind first, but rodents include chipmunks, woodchucks, and beavers.

Although as different as porcupines (yes, they're rodents, too!) are from squirrels, rodents all have some characteristics in common — much the way everyone on your father's side of the family has those jagged eyebrows, and all your first cousins can carry a tune.

"What big teeth you have, grandma . . ."

A rodent's teeth are one of its most distinctive features. Rodents have a single pair of incisors in each jaw. These long, sharp teeth (which look a little like the claws of a hammer) continue to grow throughout the animal's life and are worn down by chewing.

 Between a rodent's incisors and molars is a handy gap called a *diastema,* which allows him to store food or housing materials (like dirt or wood) before his powerful jaws push those materials back to be ground down by the molars.

Family values

It's a tough life being a small, furry object out in the wild, waiting to be some predator's lunch. (Birds of prey dine regularly on rodents.) For this reason, many rodent species become sexually mature very early (in some cases in as little as a few weeks). They also have large litters to ensure the survival of, if not the fittest, at least the mostest! (I talk about how to control your family of hamsters in Chapter 7.)

Rodents also nurse their young, another distinctively mammalian characteristic. This behavior helps make them seem affectionately familiar to us, even as we marvel at what is so different about them.

Not just a rodent

Let's face it: The word *rodent* doesn't exactly inspire warmth and affection. Instead, it makes homeowners think of hidden messes and ruined wiring, and it gives farmers visions of ruined crops. But domestic hamsters have lots of endearing attributes. For example, they're hard workers and good housekeepers — habits that they picked up in the wild.

Many species of hamsters exist, but they generally share small, stout bodies; short tails; cheek pouches (they really have that "made-for-Disney" look); and terrific burrowing abilities. Hamsters are shyer and less clever than rats or mice, but they take top honors in cuteness.

What's in a name?

As with many word origins, the ultimate source of *hamster* is disputed. However, the word may come from the Middle High German word *hamastra,* which means "to store." (This would make sense because hamsters are prodigious hoarders.) Hamsters were once known, not very accurately or politely, as *German rats.*

Although they vary somewhat according to type (especially now that they have been "customized" by breeders), hamsters share some essential traits — things that make hamsters, well, hamsters. I discuss these traits later in the chapter, in the sections "The Hamster Five: Meet the Species" and "Sizing Them Up: The Anatomy of a Hamster."

Where Hamsters Come From: A Brief History

Chances are your hamster will be called Nathan, or Doris, or Winky, or Puff Daddy, or Brittany. But he or she (I tell you how to figure out which is which in Chapter 6) is probably descended from hamsters who came from Syria, Turkey, Kazakhstan, Mongolia, or Bulgaria.

Hamsters have secretive habits: In the wild, they live in burrows anywhere from 2- to 10-feet deep. For this reason, scientists aren't quite sure when the hamster first distinguished itself as a species. However, the earliest written reference to a hamster — a Syrian Gold hamster, to be exact — appeared in 1797 (see the "World premiere: 1797" sidebar).

The Syrian Gold hamster made her next appearance in 19th-century England. This was the England of Charles Darwin, when lots of scientists and travelers were becoming interested in the natural world and anything that could be drawn, described, and dissected. One enthusiast was George Waterhouse, the curator (in 1839) of the London Zoological Society, who presented this "new" species of hamster from Aleppo (which had been written about by a fellow Englishman almost 100 years earlier). He called it *cricetus auretus.*

Traveling the road toward pethood

By the mid-19th century, hamsters had made their mark zoologically, but the next leg of their journey into our homes came quite a bit later, in the 1930s. A parasitologist working at the Hebrew University in Jerusalem, Saul Adler, was having trouble obtaining hamsters from China for his study of a fly-borne disease. He asked a colleague, Israel Aharoni, to try to capture some hamsters that were native to the region and could be bred in captivity.

Aharoni's task wasn't easy, because anxious hamsters can kill their young, and all are great escape artists. But with some difficulty he became, literally, the father of the domestic Syrian hamster. From the single litter of 11 that he found in the wild (whose offspring were delivered to Adler) descended generations of lab animals that were sent to research facilities in England, India, and eventually, the United States.

Hamsters are so prolific that, amazingly, after the 1930s no new strains of Syrian hamster were introduced into this country until an MIT graduate student, Michael Murphy, captured a dozen (eight females, four males) that started the next hamster "wave" — in 1971!

Moving from lab to lap

Hamsters may have arrived in the United States as lab animals, but these exotic charmers soon enchanted their handlers with their docility, playfulness, and beauty.

World premiere: 1797

The first written reference to a hamster appeared in the second edition of a book called *The Natural History of Aleppo* (referring to an ancient Syrian city), revised by naturalist Patrick Russell after the death of the original author, his brother Alexander.

Like many scientists of the period, Patrick evidently sought out examples of the local flora and fauna, and after excavating the stuffed pouch of what became know as the *Syrian Gold hamster*, he was astonished to discover a mass of green beans that, "when they were laid loosely on the table . . . formed a heap three times the bulk of the animal's body."

For my next trick . . .

Here's a bit of fun trivia: Parasitologist Saul Adler, responsible for the widespread dissemination of the Syrian Gold hamster, also translated Charles Darwin's *The Origin of Species* into Hebrew.

In 1948, an opportunistic Alabamian named Albert Marsh, who had won a Syrian hamster in a bet, saw the possibilities in marketing these lab animals as pets. He acted as a middleman between other small breeders and pet shop clients, and he also wrote his own hamster manual. He established the hamster as a profitable niche market in the pet industry.

The Hamster Five: Meet the Species

I mention the Syrian hamster in the previous section, but four other species of hamster are also part of the pet population: the Campbell's hamster, the Winter White or Dwarf Russian hamster, the Roborovski hamster, and the Chinese or Gray hamster. To be clear, many other species of hamsters exist in the wild, but these five are the ones you're most likely to encounter in a pet store. Not every store has a full selection, of course. Syrians still predominate, but the dwarf types are becoming quite popular, and breeders specialize in particular strains (see Chapter 3).

Just to confuse matters, some of these five species are known by common names, because the species weren't clearly distinguished when they were first identified. For example, some Syrian hamsters — those with fuzzy coats — are called *Teddy Bear hamsters,* and Winter White and Campbell's hamsters are sometimes called *Djungarian hamsters* (which does not refer to a school of psychoanalysis, by the way, but the region in Siberia where they originated).

In the following sections, I briefly describe each species. Table 1-1 offers basic information about each of the five so you can get an overview at a glance. Note that while White Whites are often formally designated as "Dwarf" hamsters, Chinese and Roborovski hamsters are also considered dwarf in some classifications.

Table 1-1	Common Pet Hamsters		
Genus	*Size*	*Weight*	*Color*
Campbell's	2–4 inches	1–2 ounces	Gray or variety
Chinese (also called *Gray*)	4–5 inches	1½–1¾ ounces	Brown with white stripe, white with brown patches, or gray with dorsal stripe
Roborovski	2–4 inches	1–1½ ounces	Gray
Syrian	4–7 inches	5–7 ounces	Golden and varieties
Winter White (also called *Dwarf Russian*)	2–4 inches	1–2 ounces	White/gray (seasonal)

Syrian Gold hamster

The hamster that started it all is the largest of the pet species, often measuring 6 to 7 inches and weighing between 5 and 7 ounces. While this hamster's color in the wild is usually golden brown with a white belly and chest (hence its official name; see Figure 1-1), the domestic Syrian now comes in as many as 20 color *morphs* (as they are known in hamster breeding circles), including black, cinnamon, and yellow, and a variety of coats, including a longhaired version that looks like an agitated starlet on her way to a movie premiere!

Figure 1-1: A Syrian Gold hamster.

Color morphs

While hamsters in the wild come in shades such as gold, gray, and brown, often with a *dorsal* (down the back) stripe, humans can never resist making a good thing better. So in captivity, hamsters have been bred to come in as many shades as fashionable fabrics, from pure white to deep sable. These variations on a theme are known as *color morphs*. I discuss color options in more detail in Chapter 3.

Syrians have longer life spans than other hamsters (see Chapter 2) and are the most easily socialized breed. Syrians are the hamsters you generally find in pet shops. They are terrific fighters among themselves, and Syrians definitely shouldn't be kept together past the age of 5 weeks.

Campbell's hamster

Despite its Scottish name, this hamster sports no tartan. Instead, it is a Mongolian native named for naturalist W.C. Campbell, who discovered it in 1902. Generally measuring 3 to 4 inches, these daintier hamsters are usually grayish (see Figure 1-2).

© Lorraine Hill, Acorn Stock Images

Figure 1-2: A Campbell's hamster.

Plump and elegant, these hamsters are more communal than Syrians by nature and can live together if they've been brought up together (the reverse of some human families).

This species might also be dubbed the "sensitive New Age hamster," because males participate in birthing and help to raise the young.

Winter White hamster

Members of this species sound like characters from an old fairy tale: They are commonly known as *Dwarf Winter White Russian hamsters*. But they are also sometimes referred to as *Siberian* or *Djungarian* hamsters.

These hamsters' coats change color with the season. In summer, they look like well-dressed businessmen, in gray suits with a dark stripe down the side (see Figure 1-3). In winter, they look more like fairy tale characters, with white or nearly white fur (see Figure 1-4). Captive Winter Whites don't always lose all their coloration, as this requires more natural light than is common to many houses or apartments. Scientists use this species for studies on how seasonality affects the brain.

Figure 1-3: A Winter White hamster with its summer coat.

Figure 1-4: A Winter White hamster with its winter coat.

 The *dwarf* appellation comes from the fact that these hamsters can be as small as 2 to 4 inches. Despite their size, they cause more allergic reactions in humans than other pet hamster species. If you're sensitive to dander, dust, or pet hair, this may not be the breed for you.

These charmers are increasingly popular and another common sight at pet stores. Their rabbit-like ears and pert expressions put them out front in the cuteness stakes, but they don't exactly have a temperament to match; they can be nippy until they get to know you. Then there's the agility factor — one pet store owner describes them as "popcorn" because they're ready to bounce right out of your hand. This makes them a hoot to watch as they manipulate their exercise toys, of course.

Latin rhythms

I promise I won't quiz you, but just in case you want to know, the Latin names for the five most common pet hamsters are as follows:

- Syrian Gold hamster: *Mesocricetus auratus*
- Campbell's hamster: *Phodophus campbelli*
- Winter White hamster: *Phodophus sungorus*
- Roborovski hamster: *Phodophus roborovski*
- Chinese hamster: *Cricetulus griseus*

And if the Campbell's hamster can boast sensitive New Age males, the Winter Whites might be thought of as old hippies: Males and females share burrows with at least two members of the opposite sex!

Roborovski hamster

A latecomer to the pet market, the Roborovski hamster was discovered in 1894 by — you guessed it — a Lieutenant Roborovski. But they weren't really domesticated until the 1970s. They hail from Mongolia, China, and Russia and are native to flat, sandy areas.

These hamsters are definitely night creatures, at their liveliest from 9 to 10 p.m. They're also a little shyer than other hamsters. Their brownish-gray fur is almost electric in color and a little tousled (see Figure 1-5).

Figure 1-5: A Roborovski hamster.

Chinese hamster

This elegant breed, also referred to as the *Gray hamster,* is notable for the sleek dark stripe down its back, which stands out from its sable-colored fur (see Figure 1-6). Slenderer than some of their pudgier cousins, Chinese hamsters measure about 4 to 5 inches. (There is also a mouse-like Dwarf Chinese hamster that measures only 1 to 2 inches.) They have longer tails than other hamsters, which some scientists believe are helpful for balance in the rocky regions of their native China and Mongolia.

Figure 1-6: Chinese hamsters.

In captivity, these hamsters are exercise fiends. They probably helped to create the popular image of the hamster running constantly on a wheel. Although often sold in same-sex pairs, experts say they can actually become quite aggressive towards each other, although they are usually extremely docile with people.

What's in a name?

Some pet shops now feature the *European hamster.* This is just casual labeling and usually refers to one of the Syrian types.

Sizing Them Up: The Anatomy of a Hamster

While the preceding section demonstrates the astonishing variety that exists among the hamster species, the basic hamster chassis (see Figure 1-7) is fundamentally the same.

Body by Fisher — not

This old auto slogan, referring to sleek efficiency, doesn't quite fit our hamster friends. *Barrel-shaped* is the common adjective applied to hamsters, although the tousled coats of Teddy Bear hamsters conceal its contours and Chinese hamsters are more mouse-like. Basically, you're looking at a sleek little keg of an animal, usually ranging from 4 to 7 inches long.

Figure 1-7: All hamsters share the same basic anatomy.

Bright eyes

While we're using old-fashioned expressions, "bright as a button" is another one that fits the hamster perfectly. Indeed, their shiny eyes look almost as if they're buttons sewn onto a child's stuffed animal.

Hamsters are prey animals rather than predators, so (like horses) their eyes are set a little to the sides of their heads, and they are farsighted — the better to see you with before you can eat them. Close up, hamsters rely more on their senses of smell and hearing.

Oh my nose and whiskers!

The hamster's soft pointed nose helps her navigate the world. This triangular feature ends in a soft (usually pink) snout that the hamster uses to recognize food, friends, family (including potential mates), and danger.

In addition to relying on a keen sense of smell, hamsters also use their long whiskers almost like antennae to sense the world around them.

All ears

Hamsters' small leaf-like ears are among their most charming features, but they're not all for show. Constantly twitching, they tell the hamster about the world around him and can sense vibrations on the ground and in the air (so the hamster can identify sources of potential danger). Like dogs, hamsters can discern higher frequencies than we can.

Cheeky

One of the hamster's most distinctive features is her cheek pouches, into which an amazing amount of food can be stuffed for a rainy day. The soft elastic skin distends and enables the hamster to transfer food and bedding, as well as to show that she's fighting mad!

Teeth

The hamster's incisors are useful tools for shredding food of all sorts, fluffing up bedding and nesting material, and capturing wandering babies. They're also handy for fighting. The top pair of incisors has a little gap into which the bottom pair fits neatly.

Hipsters

One reason for hamsters' reliance on smell is that they are equipped with glands behind their ears and, on Syrian hamsters, just at the point of their hips. These glands exude distinct odors — nature's own cologne or aftershave — that help hamsters distinguish one another and know when to mark territory.

The duplex

Despite their diminutive size, hamsters, like cows, have two stomachs. The first stomach partially digests their food, which then passes to the second stomach for absorption. This handy feature allows them to process a wide range of foodstuffs, which has enabled their continued survival in an ever-changing environment and makes them easy keepers at home. (Your child doesn't like vegetables? Never fear, your hamster's here!)

Scruffy

The fleshy area behind a hamster's ears, known as the *scruff* or *nape,* doesn't have any particular function for them. However, it's tremendously useful to us (and veterinarians) because it provides a safe, efficient way to grasp a hamster without her being able to move too much. (Hamster opponents and mates take the same advantage.)

Pianissimo

If they made instruments small enough, hamsters would be great pianists. Their small, five-toed front paws are dexterous and mobile, allowing them to easily grasp and manipulate food and to climb. Their longer, kangaroo-like hind paws are flattish so that they can push off vigorously (on that exercise wheel you're going to buy, for example) and stand up in a characteristic inquisitive stance. Some breeds, like the Winter White, have paws that are more furred.

Tail (less)

The Chinese hamster has a tail about one-third the size of its body, giving it a somewhat mouse-like appearance. But that species is the exception; most hamsters' tails taper off into a small, triangular stub.

Chapter 2

Is a Hamster Your Perfect Pet?

Maybe you imagine a hamster fitting into your life as seamlessly as a book on a shelf. But this pocket pet has needs, and you want to keep these needs in mind when you're considering whether your Syrian Gold will interface with your yoga, your Dwarf Chinese will bond with your Yorkie, or your Winter White will go with your décor.

A Hamster in the House (or Apartment)

There's a reason why rodents are the third most popular domestic pet class after cats and dogs: Their dainty size and modest needs in terms of space, exercise, and food make them a practical — as well as a winning — choice for small spaces and busy lives (see Figure 2-1).

Still, hamsters aren't goldfish, content with a small bowl of water and a frond, and they also aren't Aibos (Sony's dog-shaped "entertainment robot"). You need to be ready to buy or create a real habitat for your new friend.

© Isabelle Francais

Figure 2-1: Hamsters don't require much space in your household.

You also need to live somewhere with reasonably stable, or at least controllable, temperatures. These former desert dwellers catch cold easily, and if their environment gets too cold (below about 40°F or 5°C), they start to hibernate!

Hamsters are also sensitive to bright light (too much direct sunlight is unhealthy for them) and too much noise, although they can use their bedding to put a layer of insulation between them and the world. Good air quality is a must, however: Lungs the size of postage stamps are fragile.

Outside of these basic requirements, hamsters are very adaptable, which is how they've managed to survive for so many years in all sorts of environments from deserts to steppes (which I discuss in Chapter 1). So whether your house is a split level or a studio, your hamster should be right at home.

> # Where's my space?
>
> When you bring a hamster home, you're offering him a lifetime lease. These small rodents don't adapt too easily to constant change, so you should be sure you can guarantee him a quiet place he can call his own. Constantly shifting his habitat can really take a toll on the health and serenity of a small animal.

And the same goes for apartment dwellers: Even if you feel that you barely have enough space to hang your hat and read the newspaper, you can still provide what a hamster needs, which is stability. If you're willing to commit at least one spacious surface to be a residence for your new friend, there's no reason why a hamster can't do well in an apartment — or a mobile home or camper, for that matter.

A hamster-friendly household

Hamster owners are a friendly bunch. But just because you're friendly doesn't automatically mean your house and lifestyle are (for the hamster, that is). Ask yourself these questions:

- ✔ Is there a single room or space in your house where you can play with your hamster if you decide to let her loose?

- ✔ Are you able to secure all doors and windows so she can't escape?

- ✔ Do you have any unsafe areas of the house, such as an area with tools, exposed wires, or holes?

- ✔ Are you a frequent flyer? If so, is someone reliable available to look after your hamster(s) in your absence?

- ✔ If you have other pets, are you prepared to be vigilant? (See the next section, "Eat or be eaten: Hamsters and other pets.")

- ✔ If you have children, are you prepared to be patient and vigilant? (See the section "Hamsters and children go together, but . . ." later in the chapter.)

Be sure you can answer these questions with confidence before you bring a hamster into your life.

And hamster makes three

If you have three or more pets, you may want to consider getting health insurance, which can amount to a significant savings for major expenses of the kind more often associated with cats and dogs. Most health insurance providers offer discounts for multiple pets. Two Web sites to check are Veterinary Pet Insurance, at www.petinsurance.com, and Pet Assure, at www.petassure.com.

Eat or be eaten: Hamsters and other pets

One of the more traumatic experiences of my childhood occurred when my pet hamster, Warren (don't ask), got loose and was "rescued" by one of our poodles, Raffaelo (don't ask). Raffi was a very gentle dog, who never even chewed his rubber toys, and he picked up this new furry toy carefully in his jaws so he could put it with the rest of his treasures. Unfortunately, Warren, not realizing that he was in good hands (or jaws), died of fright.

All of which is to say that it doesn't take a lot to damage a hamster, and most other pets are likely to be less meticulous than my poodle. Hamsters are prey animals in the wild (see Chapter 1), and your dog/cat/parrot/ferret is likely to have the same views about them in your house or apartment. And even if, like Raffi, they only want to play, they're too big to play safely with something who measures only 4 inches and weighs a few ounces.

If your hamster escapes, be sure to isolate your other animals until you've rescued him, or they will be tempted to "help."

You've probably figured this out already, but it's very important to bring the message home to your children that hamsters and other pets don't mix. Kids are *(a)* curious and *(b)* optimists, and they may be tempted to experiment with inter-pet relations.

Hamsters and children go together, but . . .

Pets teach children love and responsibility, entertain and educate them, and become members of the family. But the decision to get a pet must be made with care.

Judging from the number of articles in local papers I've seen, this is a common scenario: Your young child is lobbying for a pet, and your resistance (the natural resistance of all parents to another layer of complexity in their lives) is breaking down. However, you feel a dog will be too much trouble, you don't like cats, your spouse doesn't like birds, and fish seem too much like science projects. So a small animal (known in the pet trade as an "exotic" and colloquially as a "pocket pet") seems ideal. Small animals are fun, they're cute, and they're not too much trouble. However, as numerous pet columnists point out, all living things require a degree of commitment from both you and your child or children, and small animals present specific challenges.

Perfect 10

While individual children mature at different rates, most pet experts agree that small animal pets are not for toddlers and tykes, and 10 has been mentioned as a good average age for your child to have a pet of his own. Unless you are prepared to shoulder most of the burden of care and to be constantly on your guard, keep this advice in mind. Very small children view animals as furry toys and can easily hurt them without meaning to.

Whose job is it?

Many classrooms have pets as a way of introducing children to other life forms and hammering home those nature science lessons in an entertaining way. If your child has had this experience at school, the first battle — understanding that hamsters require attention and care — has already been fought and won. If not, you need to reinforce this idea right from the beginning.

Be sure that your children are fully involved in selecting their hamster and in decisions about housing and toys. They should also help in choosing the hamster's location in your home and in preparing the habitat, food, and water. This gives your child a sense of importance and anticipation, and it establishes rhythms of care right from the get-go. Then be sure that (under supervision) some aspect of the hamster's care becomes your child's task each day.

Caution: Hold hamster right side up!

Very young children can't be expected to understand how easily animals can be hurt, but older children should be carefully shown how to stroke, hold, and play with their new friends (see Figure 2-2). I review these techniques in more detail in Chapter 6. This is especially important with hamsters, who need gentle handling to bond with their humans. Otherwise, they can get cranky (and show it with their teeth!) or frightened. Don't let this deter you, though: Almost all animals have instinctive responses to roughness and aggression, and earning the trust of an animal can make a child excited and proud.

© Isabelle Francais

Figure 2-2: Show your child how to safely play with a hamster.

Mommy, he's boring!

My guess is that a frustrated hamster owner probably created the Japanese anime series "Hamtaro: Little Hamster, Big Adventures," which was launched in the United States in 2002. Your hamster is more likely to have small adventures — running on his wheel, playing in tubes and tunnels, and sculpting his bedding.

Not the United Nations (or, just like the United Nations)

It's not just cats and dogs you have to worry about in terms of assuring your hamster's safety. Universal brotherhood does not exist among rodent species. Rats are especially aggressive toward others, and ferrets are mischievous, as well as being partial carnivores. If you want to play with your hamster Hamlet, do so in a room of his own; hold him very carefully on your lap; or place him on a soft, flat surface like a bed when other pets are not in the picture.

Endearing exotics

According to a survey conducted by the American Pet Products Manufacturers Association, 82 percent of hamster owners said the greatest benefit to having this small animal pet is the fun of watching it; 77 percent said that hamsters are good for children and teach responsibility; and 69 percent cited companionship and affection as the top benefit.

And while hamsters are happy to bond with a gentle owner and enjoy being handled and carried a little, they are not as snuggly as guinea pigs or as extroverted and clever as ferrets. As with fish, your child will have to derive some fun from watching the private life of your pet and from admiring her nimbleness and beauty.

Sleepy Heads

Hamsters are nocturnal, meaning that they're at their busiest at night and like to snooze through a good deal of the day. Their behavior patterns have altered to some extent in response to our daily rhythms and artificial lights, so hamsters — a little like cats — may have several waking and sleeping cycles during the day. (Hamsters' sleep patterns have actually been used to study the effects of sleep deprivation and alterations of the biological "clock" in humans.)

A hamster's daytime waking cycles may be punctuated by vigorous exercise, assuming that you, being a good parent, have provided the right toys (see Chapter 4). However, by and large, most of a hamster's activity takes place at night. If you want to interact with him, you need to be ready to look away from your favorite television show or your simmering pot roast to spend a little quality time with Penfold.

If you live in a small apartment or studio, you need to bear these nocturnal habits in mind because your ham may be in the mood for a stimulating run on her exercise wheel just as you're ready to catch some ZZZs. (Well-made accessories help keep down the clatter, but you still want to be sure you can live with a little low-level noise at night.)

Do not disturb

Your hamster's antics will be touching and fun — only miniature poodles and prairie dogs look this cute on their hind legs (and prairie dogs don't make good pets). But she won't have much fun at all if you're always tapping on her cage or picking her up when she's just settled in for a nice nap. (Imagine being on an airplane with a stewardess who constantly wakes you up to ask if you're comfortable!) Encourage everyone in your household to respect her napping needs, which is not only considerate, but may save you from getting nipped by a startled pet.

Even while sleeping, hamsters are fun to watch, as they tuck their contented little faces into their paws or burrows. (Admit it, isn't it nice to see that someone's getting some sleep?) But the waking hours are important for handling and socializing your hamster. As I discuss in Chapter 6, hamsters "speak" with their bodies — this is how they tell you if they're hungry, anxious, or sick. You want to be sure you have enough time at night to check for messages.

Hammy, I Hardly Knew Ye: Lifespan

A hamster can live between two and five years, depending on its size, breed, and general health. Most sources put the average lifespan around three years. You — and your offspring — need to be prepared for a short, sweet acquaintance. Unlike a dog or cat, a hamster isn't going to watch your toddler become a college graduate.

Just as pets help to teach children about the importance of all living things, so, too, they may be a child's first experience of death. Because of the short lifespan, every hamster owner has to come to terms with saying goodbye. Be prepared to explain things clearly to your child and to find ways to make the inevitable acceptable.

Children are natural ritualists, and many a story has been written about the peculiar, heart-wrenching charm of pet burials, as complete with honors and the symbols of a life well lived as any Egyptian Pharaoh could boast.

Whatever you do, do *not* make a hamster's size an excuse to dispose of it as if it were waste. Be sure everyone gets a chance to say goodbye.

Small, Not Free

In addition to their compact size and pleasing demeanor, hamsters are also popular for their thriftiness — or at least their ability to keep you thrifty. A hamster is not a big drain on your budget.

Supply costs

Table 2-1 shows how much you can expect your initial outlay to be, as well as how much it costs to keep your hamster fed and cared for in the long run. My figures come from reviewing prices at major pet supply retailers. I offer a range of typical prices, but remember that you can also comparison shop on the Internet. Dozens of sites are available, from major pet chains like Petco to small suppliers of specialty goods. (Check out my list of hamster Web sites at the end of this book, because such sites often link to retailers.)

For items such as food and bedding, I list the price for a single purchase; keep in mind that you'll be spending that much every week or two, depending on the quantities you buy. (Bedding prices vary by size/weight; a package can run from 2 pounds to 5 cubic feet.) See Chapter 4 for much more information about supplies.

Table 2-1	Hamster Expenses
Item	*Price Range*
Cage	$25–30
Food bowl	$3–4
Water bottle	$6–8
Litter/bedding	$9–14
Food (2- or 4-pound bags)	$4.50–6.50
Chew treats	$3–4 each
Toys	$4.50–6.50 each
Hideaway/den	$6.50–7.50
Tunnel	$4.50–5.50
Exercise wheel	$12–13
Nesting material	$4–6.50

Most larger pet supply stores feature a variety of hamster starter kits, which can be very good values. These kits usually include a habitat; an initial supply of bedding, food, and treats; and a water bottle, a food dish, and a toy. Depending on how splendid the habitat is, these kits run from about $26 to over $50.

A consumer survey by the American Pet Products Manufacturers Association estimates that annual expenses for owners of one hamster are $132 for people who shop in pet stores and $155 for people who shop primarily in superstores. Note that these are averages only; superstores often offer very good values compared to boutique pet stores. The higher costs are primarily for food, which probably means shoppers at pet stores are buying in bulk.

What about his shots?

I don't include an average cost for veterinary bills in this book because, unlike cats and dogs, hamsters do not need specific vaccinations or boosters and are not generally exposed to fleas or ticks. However, as I discuss in Chapter 7, many hamster health issues require immediate professional intervention, so be sure you're able to foot the bill in an emergency.

Oh, yes — the hamster!

Hamsters in pet stores list between $9 and $15. Breeders' prices vary widely, but you can expect to pay a little more to a breeder, especially if you are buying a hamster with a pedigree or one that has been especially bred for unusual color traits. (In Chapter 3, I discuss purchasing hamsters from pet stores and breeders.)

Twice the fun, twice the money

Most hamsters are solitary, except when they're breeding. If you're thinking it would be fun to have two, or if you're considering breeding (see Chapter 7), you need a separate habitat and supplies for each hamster. While these purchases still won't break the bank, they can add up. (And, of course, having two habitats doubles the challenge of setting aside personal space for your pets.)

Chapter 3

Selecting a Hamster

· ·

In This Chapter

▶ Deciding where to shop

▶ Considering a wealth of options

▶ Being an educated consumer

· ·

There's no greater pleasure, I think, than anticipating the purchase of a pet. As pet author Mordecai Siegal put it, "It's the one opportunity we have to choose a member of the family."

To make the best possible hamster choice for you and your family, you want to consider a number of points. In Chapter 1, I introduce you to the common hamster breeds; in this chapter, I help you consider these breeds as potential pets. Within each breed, a rich variety of colors and coats is available. (Are you beginning to feel as if you're in a department store?) You also need to consider the hamster's age and sex.

So, what will your choice be? A luxuriant chocolate Syrian? A nimble Chinese? A cuddly Teddy Bear? Only orchids and cupcakes come in as many varieties as hamsters.

Hamster Hunting: The Best Places to Look and Shop

Your decision about where to look for your new friend is dictated by the usual factors:

✔ **Money:** This isn't a significant issue unless you're planning to show or breed your hamster.

✔ **Time:** Do you need instant gratification, or do you want to do a little comparison shopping? (I advise the latter; keep reading for my reasons why.)

✔ **Patience:** Are you interested enough in the various breeds and many varieties (among the Syrians and Campbell's, at least) to do some research (including, of course, reading this book!) and seek out breeders?

✔ **Interest:** Is there a possibility that you may want more than a charming pet? If you're planning to breed or show your hamsters, you may want to seek out hamsters that are unusually marked and meet more exacting physical standards than simply being in good health. This brings us back to the issue of patience.

Wherever you lie on this spectrum, you want to take the time to make a wise and satisfying pick. The following sections discuss things to bear in mind about the various sources for hamsters.

Pet shops

Concerns that can arise when purchasing cats or dogs from pet stores — that they may be the product of abusive "mills" — are not, happily, present in the hamster world. Rodents are designed by nature to breed often, and commercial breeders have an investment in being responsible for their charges: With a crowded market, being able to guarantee sound, attractive animals is a plus. You should be able to find a healthy, happy hamster at your local pet store. Here is what to look for:

✔ Are hamsters (unless they are babies) in separate cages? Hamsters are basically solitary and will begin to *(a)* fight or *(b)* breed upon maturity if they are not separated.

✔ Do the shop and the hamster cages look clean and well maintained? Hamsters that come from crowded, dirty conditions are not only more likely to be susceptible to disease but may also be timid, lethargic, or aggressive and less easy to care for and socialize.

✔ Does the staff seem knowledgeable and able to help you select a breed and variety?

✔ Are the hamsters identified by breed and sex? Some shops clearly don't know much more about hamsters than you do; you can spy an offender if its signs don't say much more than "adults" or "babies."

✔ Will the staff allow you to hold the hamsters?

If the answer to any of the above questions is negative, try another pet store. You may find a different atmosphere and level of expertise at each location. (Chain stores do have an advantage over many sole proprietors, though, because they usually have institutionalized hiring and training programs and more consistent policies about purchasing, maintaining, and displaying pets.)

Beware of special sales because, as with any discounted stock, this usually means that the animals are older. Two-for-one offers are especially suspect because it means that the store doesn't know enough, or care enough, about hamster behavior to realize that they're not natural mixers.

Some pet shops "throw the hamster in" with the purchase of an aquarium. While this suggests a depressingly commodity-oriented approach to living creatures, the practice is common enough that it doesn't necessarily mean anything is wrong with the "freebies."

Breeders

Commercial breeders are essentially mass marketers who do most of their business with the retail pet segment. If you are interested in buying from a breeder, what you're looking for is a *hobbyist, show,* or *private* breeder who sells mostly to other enthusiasts. The advantages in buying from a breeder include the following:

- ✔ A breeder has intimate knowledge of the breed(s) on offer.
- ✔ A breeder keeps detailed family histories of each hamster, which has been bred for positive attributes such as health, conformation, color, and temperament.
- ✔ The hamsters are born into a more intimate and personal environment. This gives young hamsters an advantage in terms of physical conditions and sociability, as breeders tend to handle young hamsters more often than pet store employees.
- ✔ You gain an immediate entrée into the hamster community, which may be useful if you are embarking on a breeding and showing career yourself.

You may find that a breeder's prices are a little higher than a pet store's. However, many breeders are happy to sell pet quality animals for less. *Pet quality* does not indicate any kind of profound defect in the animal (although kindhearted breeders do try to find homes for deformed animals, too). The term just indicates that the hamster is not likely to be a winner in a show ring or the breeder's first choice to start a hamster dynasty!

Breeder notices

Here's what a typical breeder notice looks like. This particular one was posted on www.petwebsite.com, but you may find something similar in the classified section of your newspaper or in magazines such as The Critter Exchange (www.critter exchange.com) and Loving Pets (www.lovingpetsmagazine.com).

Syrian Hamsters

Above all, I am a hamster hobbyist. I breed for temperament, but I also breed for show qualities. Syrian Hamsters for sale in a variety of colors. Shipping available to serious breeders.

Ask for prices, California, USA

Shelters/rescues

Small animals are as much the victims of pet overpopulation as the more highly publicized dogs and cats, but overburdened, under-funded shelters can't always devote the time or space to rodents that they do to larger animals. Still, if you'd like to do a good deed at the same time that you acquire a new friend, you may want to start with a shelter.

You can also check with your local hamster clubs because some have rescue operations, or at least Web sites, usually managed by some kind soul with a conscience who would be glad to hear from you. Unlike cats or dogs, rescue hamsters are unlikely to be ill or have personality disorders; they are more often the victims of relo-cation, divorce, or loss of interest. However, they are likely to be on the older side, which is a consideration given their short life span (see Chapter 2).

Classifieds

Open any paper in the country or the suburbs, and you'll find people selling, or giving away, everything from tractors to terra-pins. Except for advertisements placed by breeders, most classi-fied listings for hamsters are likely to fall in the "free to a good home" category and will be the result of some lifestyle dislocation.

A hamster acquired from a former owner is likely to be on the mature side, but one plus is that he may also come with all the accoutrements and be a proven pet success in at least one family. However, the disadvantage is that rodents are sensitive to changes in atmosphere and environment. (Wouldn't you be, if you'd spent centuries keeping one step ahead of civilization?) Change can sometimes be traumatic or at least disorienting, making it more difficult for hamsters to bond with new people or settle comfortably in new places.

Each hamster is different, and before you make a choice to take one home, you want to measure her temperament. I explain how to do so in the section "Shopping Like a Pro," later in this chapter.

Online

You can now shop for hamsters, as you can shop for almost every other commodity, over the Internet. But use the same kind of caution that you would with any other Web-based purchase. Be sure to either talk to a human being or exchange enough messages to have some guarantee that the site is genuine and the establishment reputable. Be on the lookout for impromptu dealers who don't know much about hamsters.

The Internet Hamster Association of North America (IHANA) has adopted a code that it asks all professional breeders to adhere to, including provisions about the responsible choice of breeding stock and disposition of litters. The code can be reviewed at `http://groups.msn.com/InternetHamsterAssoc/breederscode.msnw`. You may want to ask any breeder you meet online if he is familiar with IHANA.

Schoolrooms

Many schools use animals to help children learn about other creatures and how to care for them. Depending on the nature of the programs in your area, a school may cycle animals through and be looking to place a hamster after its turn as class mascot is over. Or schools may need to find summer homes for class projects at the end of the school year.

If your child starts agitating for a hamster, check to see what's currently in his classroom. Schoolroom hamsters may be a bit older but should come with all their accessories and are likely used to being handled and showing off for an audience.

Mystery hamsters

Many a first pet has made its way into the life of a child seemingly by magic. So don't be altogether surprised to come home one day and find a hamster fully installed in your home. Where did she come from? "A man had them." "Tony had one." "They were so cute and only five dollars and I promise to take care of him." You get the idea. Even if you're able to track down the dubious pet broker, the die is probably cast and the bond formed. Unless the hamster is clearly sickly, if you try to return it, you will become the subject of many future psychotherapy sessions.

Deciding on the Right Hamster for You

Now that you know all about where to hunt for your hamster, what, exactly, are you hunting for? While the perfect pet may still choose you, having some idea of what you're looking for helps narrow the search and guarantees more pleasure later.

First, take a look at Chapter 1 to review the five major pet breeds of hamsters: Syrian, Campbell's, Winter White (or Dwarf Russian), Roborovski, and Chinese, which also come in a dwarf form. While they all share basic hamster characteristics, you need to bear their distinctive features in mind when choosing and handling your prospects.

Next, consider your other options: gender, age, coat length, and color. The following sections can help.

Male or female

If you're buying just one hamster, gender doesn't pose much of an issue because this species doesn't have many significant gender-linked traits. If you're buying more than one hamster, the gender issue takes on some significance. If you buy a boy and a girl, you will get more hamsters than you bargained for. If you buy two boys, the Battle of the Bulge (or at least of the bulging cheeks!) may break out. (See Chapter 6 for details about why angry hamsters puff their cheeks.)

So if you want more than one hamster, make sure you select a communal breed — which leaves out Syrians because they like to fight among themselves — and be sure you can tell the Harrys from the Harriets. See Chapter 6 for guidance on sexing your hamster, or ask the pet shop assistant to help you; gender IDs are part of basic training at most pet stores.

Age

We all want our pets to have perpetual youth. However, hamsters have relatively short life spans, so you may want to acquire a baby, or at least a young hamster. Baby hamsters are fairly easy to recognize: They are smaller, of course, and usually have that slightly rubbery, unformed look.

Hamsters mature at about 5 weeks and shouldn't be sold much younger than that. Breeders can tell you the exact age of their offerings, and most hamsters in pet shops can be presumed to be relatively young because the stock should turn over quickly. Some can be as old as 3 to 4 months, though.

You can't always tell a hamster in dapper middle age, but you should be vigilant for signs of real age — such as patchy fur, thinness, and a lack of curiosity. (These may also be symptoms of sickness, as I explain in the upcoming section "Inspecting a hamster's health.")

All this being said, if you decide to find your first hamster at a shelter or a school, accept the fact that this will probably be a mature fellow, and enjoy him accordingly.

A Teddy by any other name

The Syrian long-haired hamster is often called the Teddy Bear hamster, and you will frequently see this name, instead of the designation "Syrian," on cages in pet shops. (No doubt pet shop owners want to cash in on what's cuddly!)

Hamster hair days

Hamsters come with four basic coat types: hairless, normal or short-coated (the most common), long-haired, and satin. A more exotic variation also exists (in both short-coated and long-haired hamsters) called *rex,* in which the coat curls upwards.

- **Hairless:** This coat type is also called *alien,* and for good reason. These furless hamsters have transparent skins and the slightly synthetic look of most hairless breeds. And like other hairless critters, they are more susceptible to temperature shifts and to their environments generally.

- **Normal or short-coated:** This is your standard-issue hamster, with short, dense fur that lies relatively close to the body, giving hamsters that furry dirigible look that is so endearing.

- **Long-haired:** Long-haired hamsters can be quite dramatic, with luxuriant fluffy coats that look almost like Angoras (see Figure 3-1). While hamsters are assiduous groomers, most sources recommend a little grooming of long-haired hamsters, as their bedding tends to stick to them! (Grooming is also a nice, nurturing way to spend time with your friend.)

This coat style is common to Syrians and has led to them also being referred to as *Teddy Bear* hamsters, though this is really a colloquial description of the coat rather than the breed.

- **Satin:** This look is almost exactly what it sounds like: coats with extra sheen on them. Depending on the breed of hamster, some satin coats are as sleek as platinum, and others have a slightly disheveled look, as if a hairdresser has moussed them.

- **Rex:** Syrian rex-coated hamsters look as if they're wearing a cross between fake fur coats and pile carpeting (see Figure 3-2). A relatively recent import to North America, this coat can appear with many different color varieties and is sometimes confused with other wavy-coat patterns. The deciding factor, say breeders, is that rex-coated hamsters have curly whiskers as well, bending inward like the moustaches of old-fashioned stage villains.

Adding all the coat and color types together, more than 120 varieties of hamster exist, so you definitely have some options to consider.

Figure 3-1: A long-haired hamster.

Figure 3-2: A hamster with a rex coat.

Coats of many colors

Hamster coat colors are where art and nature mix. From the basic gold, brown, gray, and white of the common hamster breeds, fanciers have created a palette of colors (especially for the Syrian and Campbell's hamsters) that range from pure white to ink black, with dazzling shades like cream, yellow black, lilac, cinnamon, smoke pearl, and copper. Hamster coat colors also dictate eye color, which can be black or red.

In addition, differing coat patterns, some involving marks, are also common. These include tortoiseshell (see Figure 3-3), roan, banded, piebald, and dominant spot. (Many of the Web sites I suggest in the list at the back of this book contain photos that can help you visualize coat patterns.) While sources agree on some common designations, all caution that hamster breeders are like rose gardeners — always happy to believe they've created something new and to name it accordingly. If you want a particular color and pattern and you are ordering your hamster from a breeder, don't settle for sight unseen — get a photo.

© Lorraine Hill, Acorn Stock Images

Figure 3-3: A hamster with a tortoiseshell pattern.

After you've familiarized yourself with the lovely color choices, do not be surprised to find none of them at your local pet store, or at least to find the labeling more reductive. Pet stores do not cater to would-be breeders or serious hamster aficionados, and they often label their specimens according to coat type rather than color.

Table 3-1 lists some common coat colors for the major breeds. Sources vary; this list is derived from Lorraine Hill, a British pet author.

Table 3-1		Common Colors for Hamster Breeds
Breed	*Color*	*Description*
Syrians	Golden	The original Ford of hamsters — a mustardy color with a dark line over the shoulders and dark gray at the roots
	Black	Also called *sable* because the underbelly is lighter and the color is actually a mutation of the golden
	Cinnamon	Spicy ginger with a blue-gray underbelly
	Cream	Especially pretty shades, with pink or cream undertones
	Gray	Comes in both light and dark shades, as well as a silver with darker roots
	Pearl smoke	Glamorous, with pale gray fur at the root, a darker shade at the surface, and an ivory belly
	Lilac	Gray fur with lavender undertones and an ivory belly
	Yellow	Also described as *tan;* like the Mustang horse of the Old West
	Yellow-black	A sort of hamster bumblebee — yellow fur with black tips and gray ears
Campbell's	Normal	Grayish brown with a dark dorsal stripe. Can also be *normal with mottling,* meaning there are white patches throughout the coat, or *normal with platinum,* meaning white hairs are evenly distributed.
	Argente	Described as like cinnamon (which is a coat color in its own right) and ginger, with a blue underbelly. Also comes in a mottled variety.
	Beige	A dreary word, but a lovely color of pale orange with a dark dorsal stripe
	Black	More like a two-toned shoe, as the feet and chin are white

(continued)

Table 3-1 _(continued)_

Breed	_Color_	_Description_
Campbell's	Blue	Gray-blue fur with a dark stripe. Blues also come in _mottled_ and _fawn,_ which is an odd mix of blue and tan (like an old convertible).
	Opal	Blue-gray with an ivory belly and snout area (unique to Campbell's). Also has mottled and platinum varieties.
	Albino	As with Syrians, an interesting strain created by breeders

Breeders seem to have focused their color and coat experiments on Syrians and Campbell's; Roborovski and Chinese hamsters have remained essentially as nature designed them, and Winter Whites are of course defined by their color, which changes to a mottled gray in summer (see Chapter 1).

If you're in the market for an albino Syrian or Campbell's hamster, keep in mind that they are prone to diabetes.

Shopping Like a Pro

If you buy from a breeder, you'll probably get closer supervision than if you're surveying the field at a pet store. In either case, you want the opportunity to hold your prospect (or two or three of them). Even if the establishment is somewhat _laissez faire,_ be sure that someone is on hand just in case the hamster makes a bid for freedom (remember that popcorn analogy?).

Getting hands-on

Hamsters are not fine china, and you're buying a friend and companion, not a collectible. If a breeder or pet store staff member won't let you handle the hamsters, move on.

Breeders almost always encourage people to hold their animals, but you may encounter some resistance at the pet store. If the person helping you is young or seems uncertain, she may not feel she has the authority to let you touch the animals, so ask for the manager.

Most hamsters are kept — either alone or communally — in a cage with a lid that can be removed from above so you can reach in and scoop out the little Dwarf Russian whose bright eyes appealed to you, or test the pleasing heft of a larger Syrian. Hold the hamster gently, and stroke it. See if you can get a sense of how relaxed or inquisitive the hamster is. This is also a good time to check out its general health (see the upcoming section "Inspecting a hamster's health") and, of course, its gender.

Finding Miss (or Mr.) Congeniality

Color and coat are certainly intriguing, but personality may be more important than both. Syrians are the easiest hamsters to socialize, although I'm not suggesting that you reject other breeds for this reason. Even Winter Whites, which tend to nip, are worth considering. (Their tiny teeth can't really do much damage to you anyway!) Chapter 1 provides information about the temperament of each breed.

Like many animals, hamsters sometimes nip when they're nervous or feel cornered. You are likely to meet hamsters on the defensive in a pet shop, so don't be put off by a nip or two. Of more concern is a hamster who seems really timid or terrified; few are immediately cuddly, but hamsters who cower or shy away may be very difficult to socialize and possibly even unhealthy.

While hamsters are less likely than puppies or kittens to snuggle, you are still looking for that indefinable bond, and you'll know when you've found it.

Inspecting a hamster's health

As with any animals (including humans), *healthy* is defined for hamsters in both physical and mental terms. When you examine hamsters as possible pets, you are looking for telltale signs that all is not well — or, to put it more cheerfully, you're looking for the best and brightest hamster you can find. Unless you are planning to start a rescue operation, don't feel bad about taking this approach. Few things are sadder than attaching yourself (or, worse, having your children attach themselves) to an animal that is sick or dying.

Body beautiful

Here are the signs of health that you're looking for:

- ✔ **Teeth:** A hamster's teeth should be properly aligned, meaning that the longer top incisors should just overlap the lower teeth (see Figure 3-4). This positioning guarantees that the hamster's teeth will wear away gradually. Crooked teeth prevent this, making it hard for the hamster to chew properly or to tuck food away in her pouches.

  Hamsters with *malocclusion* have misaligned jaws that make it difficult for them to process food properly. In extreme cases, they can starve to death.

- ✔ **Eyes:** A hamster's eyes should be bright, with no redness around the eyes or discharge. (Keep in mind that the eyes themselves may be red; some hamsters have bright ruby eyes.)

- ✔ **Nose:** You want it to be dry. Wet noses are healthy in dogs and cats but not in hamsters.

- ✔ **Fur:** Depending on the coat type, hamster fur can be sleek or tousled, but either way it should have the sheen of healthy hair, and there should be no bald patches.

- ✔ **Skin:** It's important to ask to hold hamsters when you're shopping because not much of a hamster's skin is evident to the eye. When you hold him, run your hands lightly over his body (which he'll like, as long as you're gentle), and be sure the skin feels smooth and supple. If the skin feels scaly, that can signal a fungal disorder, such as ringworm, or a parasite problem. Also check for lumps and bumps; like all mammals, hamsters are prone to tumors and cysts when they are older.

- ✔ **Tail:** The tail is one of the most crucial things to check. Hamsters are susceptible to a serious condition called *wet tail,* which is fatal 80 percent of the time. If you see any sign of dampness or diarrhea in the nether region, immediately report it to the pet shop manager or breeder (who should know better), because the condition is also highly contagious.

- ✔ **Weight:** You've probably admired the sweet photos of hamsters in this book, so you know that a healthy hamster is like a little dumpling. Even the smaller Dwarf Russian, Robovorski, and Chinese hamsters are tapered, not gaunt. Boniness in a hamster may denote illness or, at least, advanced age.

- ✔ **Posture/action:** You want your hamster to be loose and energetic, like a cross between a ball and a ballet dancer. If the hamster is holding herself uncomfortably or rigidly, or if she remains curled up when she's awake, this is a sign of damage or pain. (Again, be sure to point this out to any staff.)

Figure 3-4: Properly aligned teeth are a sign of health.

A beautiful mind

I talk earlier in the chapter about hamster temperament. Feistiness is not grounds for rejection, but dullness, inattention, or fearfulness is. All experts agree: A hamster's leading characteristics are abundant energy and insatiable curiosity. Any animal who's not saying "Welcome to my world!" may not be long for this one.

Chapter 4

C'mon In: Setting Up Your Hamster's Home and Getting Him There Safely

*C*reating a home for your hamster is like creating your own *diorama* — a fascinating display like the ones in museums where you can watch animals interact in a miniature ecosystem. Although they are classed as *pocket pets,* hamsters could as easily be called *performance pets,* ready to enjoy life right in front of you.

You have three goals in choosing hamster housing and accessories: ensuring the health and safety of your pet, pleasing and entertaining her, and selecting items that are convenient for you. This chapter offers some guidelines for designing the perfect hamster habitat and getting your new friend home safely.

Home, Sweet Hamster

Caging and bedding choices are partly designed to compensate your pet for taking him out of the wild, even if that happened 400 years ago, because hamster brains are still patterned after the behavior of their ancestors. Housing should be roomy enough to allow for play, as well as for bedtime.

Housing options

The most common types of hamster housing are aquariums, standard cages, and commercially designed habitats. Each has advantages and disadvantages.

Aquariums

If you buy your hamster from a pet shop, you'll probably meet him in this type of display (see Figure 4-1). Ten gallons is considered the minimum comfortable size for a single hamster, and you may want to think about going a size larger if you are getting a Syrian; their generous proportions look a little cramped in small aquariums.

Figure 4-1: An aquarium makes a good hamster home.

The aquarium should have a meshed screen on top to prevent escape or exploration by your other household pets, and to allow for airflow through an otherwise solid container. Pet stores usually sell screens separately for five to ten dollars. They should be tightly woven, as a scampering hamster can otherwise easily catch one of his toes.

Here are some advantages of using an aquarium:

- ✔ You can see through the glass so you can watch your hamster television easily.
- ✔ They're easy to clean and not smelly.
- ✔ They keep bedding and other flotsam and jetsam of active hamster life fully contained.

Disadvantages include the following:

- ✔ Glass, and even flat plastic, accentuates temperatures, so these enclosures can become quite hot and even dangerous in direct sunlight. (This means you aren't going to place an aquarium there, right?)

- ✔ Hamsters are not fish, content to float dreamily in their own worlds. They want to smell and touch yours, and aquariums keep them from doing so.

- ✔ Some of the nifty hamster accessories (see the "Playtime" section later in the chapter) work better with cages, which have more places to hang things.

Cages

Basic slatted cages are available for all classes of small rodent. Hamster cages should have slats no wider than one-half inch, or your personal Houdini will be on his way in the blink of an eye. (If you're planning to breed, or if you become a grandmother/father unexpectedly, you need to have even thinner slats or line the lower levels of the cage with plastic inserts, thin wood, or cardboard until the babies are mature.)

A cage for a single hamster should measure at least 24 x 18 x 12 inches, and it should have some kind of set-in tray so that your hamster won't hurt or catch his feet clutching at uncomfortable bars. The alternative style features a plastic base on which the cage structure is placed and secured by fastenings or grooved notches. You can also buy split-level cages (think of gorilla cages at the zoo), which allow your hamster more fun and mobility. Most cages come with latched doors on the tops or sides, and some have a hollowed-out area for you to hang your hamster's water bottle.

The advantages of using a cage include the following:

- ✔ The airflow is better than in an aquarium.
- ✔ A cage is easier to hook water bottles and accessories to than an aquarium.

But here are some disadvantages:

- ✔ Bedding and odors can drift from the cage to surrounding areas.
- ✔ Latched gates are an invitation to these escape artists.
- ✔ Slats offer slightly more risk of catching vulnerable toes, and they can be hazardous to exploring babies.
- ✔ Cages aren't very aesthetically pleasing.

Hamster condominiums

Real estate agents aren't the only ones making a killing on the market. Pet manufacturers have created a wide variety of "critter" (as they seemed determined to call them) habitats with lots of built-in features. These habitats are usually plastic and look like kinetic sculptures, Rube Goldberg cartoons, or 1950s jukeboxes.

Features such as exercise wheels and tube tunnels are set in to the habitat's main structure, and additional attachments are often available (sort of like your vacuum cleaner). Some habitats also have built-in water bottles.

The advantages of these hamster condos include the following:

✔ You get one-stop shopping because the cage comes with many of the accessories you'd want to buy anyway.

✔ They imitate a hamster's natural habitat, allowing her to play and use her imagination freely.

✔ They're fun to look at.

But there are disadvantages:

✔ Assembly is definitely required.

✔ The habitats can be hard to clean — the system must be deconstructed so you can reach every part, and then put back together again.

✔ Plastic is edible, and your hamster will try to eat it, which may cause injury or permit escape.

✔ Did I mention that they look like 1950s jukeboxes? This may not be your design scheme of choice.

Starter kits

Many larger pet stores and chains now offer hamster *starter kits,* which typically include a cage, bedding, a commercial feed, a toy, a treat, a water bottle, and a food dish. The more modest kits (in the $25–$32 range) usually have small cages, which are perfectly adequate for a single hamster. Cages in the larger kits (which can run up to $45–$55) are often deluxe, with two levels.

Starter kits are a good buy if you like the idea of using a cage, because you will probably pay less than you would if you bought each item individually.

I love what you've done with the place: Bedding and other basics

Hamsters are long-distance sleepers, so their sleeping arrangements are very important to them. The bedding you place in your hamster's home should help her feel comfy and secure, and it should minimize your chores.

Substrate

Before we get to bedding options, a quick vocabulary lesson: A *substrate* is a layer of matter that lies under any other layer. In cages, a substrate is used to protect the base and to help absorb odor and moisture. Some substrates make good bedding, but bedding can also be deeper and needs to be comfortable for sleeping and burrowing.

Some people distinguish between substrate and bedding, and some don't — most bedding materials can serve either function.

Bedding

The popularity of rodent pets has assured that many bedding varieties are on the market, each with advantages and disadvantages. Here are some common types of bedding materials:

- ✔ **Wood shavings:** Wood shavings are economical and easy to come by. Keep an eye out for large splintery pieces when pouring this bedding into your cage or aquarium — sometimes this material isn't fully processed. Shavings come from various woods, usually the cheaper end of the market. Aspen, pine, and cedar are common, and the first two are fine, though pine shavings are very dusty.

    You should *never* use cedar shavings for your hamster. Cedar naturally exudes aromatic oils called *phenols,* but the very thing that makes cedar appealing to us is potentially fatal to hamsters, especially because they are inhaling the fumes constantly.

- ✔ **Wood pulp:** Pulp is more environmentally correct and hamster-aware than wood shavings. Pulp looks a little like minutely shredded cabbage, and the brands I've seen recently hasten to assure you that they are "free from aromatic hydrocarbons" (the dangerous phenols I discuss in the previous bullet). Pulp is very absorbent but not as easy for hamsters to sculpt as wood shavings, so you may want to give your friend something else to play with if you buy this. Pulp is priced a bit higher than shavings.

- **Pellets:** Although usually made from wood, pellets are sometimes compressed vegetable or grain byproducts, such as wheat grass. Pellets are usually efficient odor absorbers and are economical because they are concentrated and designed to break down. After they break down, however, they lose their absorbency and become damp sawdust or sludge, which may mean cleaning the cage a little more often that you'd like.

- **Corncobs:** No, your hamster isn't going on a Fourth of July picnic every day of the year. These cobs have been ground down to a fine, granulated form that looks like ancient Mayan maize and is an attractive shade of mustard. However, this material is not very absorbent, is tempting for your hamster to ingest, and occasionally suffers from mold.

- **Hay or straw:** Hay or straw is a useful bedding supplement because its pleasing tufts encourage hamsters to nest. However, if you use too much of it, they sometimes have a hard time distinguishing bed from breakfast.

- **Shredded paper:** This is useful emergency bedding. Shredded newspaper, paper toweling, or plain paper can be used temporarily, but don't let your instinct for thrift wed you to this approach. Paper gets damp easily and, with the exception of paper toweling, doesn't absorb well. Commercial paper is sometimes coated for resilience, which doesn't make it very comfortable even when shredded, and newspaper is covered in potentially toxic, or at least grubby, newsprint. The same goes for party papers like confetti, which are also not particularly economical, either.

- **Bed "fluff":** This is the hamster equivalent to throw pillows — some type of thickly wadded batting, like cotton, that the hamster can shred and play with. This is now commercially available, but you can also supply your hamster with cotton batting from your local drugstore, where it's sold in rolls.

Never use cat litter in your hamster's cage. Hamsters eat some of their feces as a way of gaining nourishment. (I know, I know, but it's a trait of the species, left over from a tough life in the wild.) The chemicals in cat litter are likely to be toxic. Also, many cat litters now have chemicals that make them clump, which can cause intestinal blockage in your pet.

Water bottles

This is possibly the most important purchase you'll make for your hamster. All animals, especially those in confined environments, need a constant supply of fresh water. And because rodents like to

do a lot of redecorating with their food and bedding, and are somewhat free in their personal habits, a water bowl isn't really practical.

Invest in a reasonably priced commercial water bottle. These bottles
are usually plastic or lightweight glass and are designed to imitate
laboratory drip bottles. They hook onto the side of a cage or can be
suspended through an opening in the top. The bottle tapers down
to a small metal funnel, where the hamster can suck the water.

You may have to play around with placement to get the bottle at the
right level for your hamster to drink. He'll let you know if you've got
it wrong by reaching for it if it's too high or bopping it if it's too low.

Food bowls

Food bowls give you a lot of hamster photo ops. You want a slightly
heavy ceramic or metal bowl, shallow enough for your hamster to
reach his food easily. No sooner will you place your attractive seed
mixture and chew toys in the bowl than your hamster will scatter it
about and sit in the bowl instead. Make sure it's big enough to allow
for this cunning habit.

You may want to get two bowls, one specifically for hay (although
this, too, usually winds up decorating your hamster's pad). Bowls
are commonly sold at pet stores, but if you want to be thrifty and
convert something of your own, a sturdy condiment dish, a shallow
small mixing bowl, or an arty ashtray (unused, please) will also work.

Temperature Control

You and your hamster can happily coexist in average room
temperatures — between 65° and 80°F. Hamsters should be kept
out of drafts and direct sunlight.

Basically, temperature control for hamsters is a matter of common
sense: If you, the dog, and the bathroom mirror are feeling the cold
or heat, so is your hamster. Beware, however, of trying to control
too many factors. Animals are usually better off being left to adjust
naturally to their surroundings, and hamsters use their bedding to
keep snug.

For breeding mothers, try to maintain a temperature of 70° to
75°F. If you have trouble maintaining this temperature through
your central heating system, you can try a small sunlamp or
portable heating fan, but don't put it too close to the cage.

Playtime

Hamsters are like children in more ways than one: All their accessories come in bold, often iridescent primary colors. If your house is done up in tasteful shades of cream, be prepared for the Technicolor invasion.

Hideaways and burrows, tunnels and funnels

A century of domestic breeding hasn't eradicated thousands of years of instinct, and one of a hamster's major instincts is to burrow and hide. In addition to fluffing up their bedding to create hiding spaces, hams enjoy objects that suggest the elaborate tunnels their ancestors in Syria and China would have carved out of sand. Some common examples of this type of product include the following:

- **Mock houses:** These are often miniature versions of your basic suburban home or two-car garage, with openings and a slanted roof.

- **Tubing:** You have many options, from adapted PVC piping to commercially manufactured plastic tunnels (see Figure 4-2) that can be placed in the cage or, in the case of hamster condominiums, attached to it.

- **Domes:** These rounded cavelike spaces usually have holes for ventilation.

- **Hollow logs:** These half logs are hollowed out like coconut shells and look like little covered bridges. Hamsters not only like to sit under them, but the bigger ones are also fond of upending them.

- **Habitat trails:** These contoured plastic trays have tunnels for running through.

Fitness freaks: Exercise wheels and balls

We may exercise so we can model this season's swimwear at the beach, but hamsters need to exercise for both health and peace of mind (see Chapter 5). Happily, the pet product community has risen to this challenge, and a wide variety of hamster sports equipment is on the market. The two main types are exercise wheels and balls.

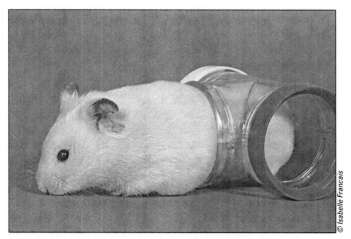

Figure 4-2: Tubing makes a great hamster hideout.

Gotta have wheels

Wheels come in a variety of styles and sizes (such as 5½ inches, 8½ inches, and 11 inches). Some are slatted, like miniature Ferris wheels. Others are made of solid plastic and are known as *comfort wheels* because the hamster doesn't have to grip with her paws to turn them, and she can rest at the base of the wheel when she's tired of running (if she's ever tired of running — hamsters can run up to 8 miles a day on an exercise wheel). A third variety is a closed wheel suspended in a wheeled frame like a plough or chariot so the hamster can actually travel around the room.

Hamster balls

Similar to the wheeled chariot, these hollowed-out plastic balls roll around the room when your hamster trots in them, so they can be used for extra fun outside of the cage.

One note of caution: These balls are enclosed spaces, so your hamster doesn't have much ventilation or access to water. He shouldn't be allowed to play in a ball for too long. If he is not your only pet, you want to place him in a room where he can experiment with this toy safely, or be sure that your other animals are secured elsewhere or out on play dates of their own!

Toys

An entire book — or at least a catalog — could be devoted to hamster toys. A wide variety of objects destined to afford the hamster hours of fun running, hiding, exploring, and redecorating are on the market.

Stuff you can buy

Hamster toys often do double duty. For example, oversized plastic fruit (in strawberry, pear, and orange shapes) with hollowed-out forms are good for a game of hide-and-seek and nice for a nap afterwards. A colorful chew stick can be tossed around and buried in a secret spot (hamsters were probably the originators of the conspiracy theory phenomenon), and it satisfies the gnawing instinct.

Most hamster toys look like educational playthings for toddlers — with bright primary colors and elemental shapes — and some of the same prohibitions apply: Toys shouldn't have any sharp edges, and wood should be untreated because your hamster's going to gnaw on it.

Some common hamster toys you can find in a pet store include:

- ✓ Geometric shapes, such as cubes, hexagons, and globes, usually made from plastic or wood. These shapes have holes and can connect to slides, tunnels, or other cubes to create a hamster jungle gym.
- ✓ Ladders
- ✓ Seesaws
- ✓ Wooden barrels
- ✓ Climbing bars so your hamster can train for the Olympics
- ✓ Bungee cords so your hamster can suspend herself in the cage. (Don't worry, she won't be swinging through your kitchen.)

Stuff you can make

Hamsters don't need personal shoppers and certainly don't know brand names. They don't care whether their fun is sophisticated and mass-produced or simple and homemade. Your house is probably already a treasure trove of potential hamster accessories and toys, and you never realized it! The only limits are safety and your own ingenuity.

The science of play

Who am I to argue with science, but I wonder if researchers who find hamsters less intelligent than rats, for example, may be measuring by the wrong standards. Hamsters are kinetically intelligent, rather than intellectually bright. (In other words, in fashionable parlance, they are right-brained, not left-brained.) They think with their bodies. Toys are designed to help them solve problems in ways that they find entertaining so they don't try to solve problems like, "How do I get the door unlatched?"

For example, here are some common household items that can be repurposed for your hamster:

- ✓ Toilet paper tubes
- ✓ Soup tins (with no sharp edges)
- ✓ Tea caddies
- ✓ Ladders from bird cages or dollhouses. (As a child, I frequently stole from my dolls to give to my pets.)
- ✓ Lego sets
- ✓ Fruit tree branches (for decoration and chewing pleasure)
- ✓ Oversized cardboard Easter eggs
- ✓ Baskets
- ✓ Wooden spools

If you're handy, or if you want to give your child a craft project, you can make your own paper chains, platforms, or tunnels. Have fun, but keep away from items with soluble dyes, anything sharp or splintery, and wood that has been treated. Also be sure that anything you make (or buy) for your hamster's home is sturdy enough to stay put and carefully secured to prevent it from coming loose and injuring your pet. And remember those teeth — wood, paper, and lightweight plastic are all vulnerable.

Not only is it fun to make a project of creating things for your hamster, but hams need a lot of variety: Experts recommend circulating toys so they have something new to think about. At five to ten dollars a pop for toys at the pet store, keeping your hamster happy can get expensive unless you get creative.

Well, You Wanted To Be a Parent: Hamster Housekeeping

Hamsters are often touted as pets with no scent, and indeed they are much less pungent than other rodents or mammals. However, unclean conditions will make themselves known and are also unhealthy for your pet.

Cleaning the bathroom

You should clean the "toilet" area of your hamster's cage daily. What is the toilet area? Hamsters are fastidious in their personal habits (try horses if you want a real contrast), and they designate one area of their cage as the bathroom. This is a good reason to get as large a cage or other habitat as you can comfortably accommodate so your hamster has room to create this separation.

In *The Hamster Handbook* (Barron's Educational Series), Patricia Bartlett suggests creating a little litter pan, similar to that used by cats, by cutting down a juice carton. This litter pan is easy to remove and, again, should be cleaned daily.

Most hamsters do not like to eat near their feces, although they do eat some of their waste as part of their survival process.

Changing the bedding

The rest of your hamster's bedding should be completely changed weekly because hamsters tend to secrete food in it, which can mold and rot. Besides, all that scampering is bound to spread waste and debris around anyway.

Some people recommend completely cleaning the cage with nonirritant detergent once a week, along with all the toys and cage or play units. I say this is a judgment call. Check to see if anything seems unpleasantly damp, soiled, or smelly, and act accordingly. In addition to fresh bedding, another good way to combat odors is to sprinkle a little baking soda at the base of the cage.

Providing temporary housing

Before you clean the cage, be sure you set up a space to temporarily house your hamster. If you have a secure room (see the next section), this may be a good time to let her romp. Otherwise, a deep wastepaper basket, plastic container, or cardboard box with a lid with holes in it should suffice; be sure you place plenty of bedding and a favorite toy or two in this container.

Remove your hamster gently from her cage, and have the new abode right beside you to plop her into — you don't want to risk escape. If you are placing your hamster in another room, have a container ready to transport her in.

Hamster-proofing Your House

Hamster-proofing takes up a lot of room in hamster articles and manuals — a sure sign that it can't be done! The best you can do is get rid of the most obvious hazards in any room in which you are planning to let your friend out to play.

To create a safe haven for your energetic, inquisitive friend, you have to use your common sense and think like a hamster. Know that hamsters have a child's unerring instinct for finding the one place you don't want them to go and the one thing you don't want them to touch. Following is your hamster-proofing checklist (which won't be foolproof, but hope springs eternal!):

- ✔ **Fill cracks in floors, in walls, and at joints in appliances.** Gaps that look miniscule to you are spacious porticos to your little Chinese hamster.

- ✔ **Move all electrical cords out of reach.** Anyone who has experienced a mouse-induced blackout knows that cords and cables are especially tempting to rodents, who view them as taffy.

- ✔ **Move anything made of wood or paper out of reach.** If you can't move it, consider spraying it with a commercial animal repellent. These sprays are available from pet and agricultural supply stores and often have hopeful names like Pet Off; Bitter Apple is also a common brand.

- ✔ **Remove plants, or place them on a very high surface.** Unless you are a veterinarian or a botanist, you won't know what may be toxic to your hamster, and he's bound to want to try out anything green and leafy.

- ✔ **Put away household cleansers or chemicals.** You probably shouldn't let your hamster out if you've just cleaned with anything chemically aggressive; hamsters have very delicate respiratory systems.

- ✔ **Close all drawers, lids, closets, bins, buckets, slats, and boxes.**

- ✔ **Turn off all burners and gas jets, and cover the slats on the toaster.**

- ✔ **Pull furniture a little bit out from the wall.** You don't want your hamster to cower out of reach or wedge himself under something.

- ✔ **Beware of loose-fitting baseboard heating covers.** This is exactly the sort of space that most appeals to a small, secretive animal, who can place himself dangerously near the heat coils and be very hard to retrieve.

- ✔ **Check for any protruding edges or sharp objects.**

There, that was simple, wasn't it? The whole point of all this effort is to allow your hamster more space to roam around, and to try to ensure his safety if he ever gets loose. One way to be sure he spends less time inventing ingenious ways to get in trouble with your possessions is to seed the room with some toys and playthings.

Hamster on Board

In an ideal world, you will have your hamster's habitat set up before you bring her home, the way new parents have the nursery all furnished and arranged before the ceremonial appearance of mother and newborn from the maternity ward.

In the real world, your hamster will probably be acquired at the same time as her paraphernalia. Assuming that your new friend is not a complete impulse buy, you should at least prepare a safe temporary abode for your hamster while you make up her suite at the Ritz.

This temporary abode can be a deep cardboard or plastic box; plastic storage bins for shoes or sweaters work well. Make holes in the lid and put in some bedding, a food dish, and a new toy. (A water bottle is harder to rig in a temporary space, and as long as the hamster's in there for less than an hour, she should be fine without it.)

When you go to select or pick up your pet, bring someone with you if you can. Top candidates are the child who lobbied most heavily for this pet (no time like the present to practice responsibility); your spouse (a useful bonding strategy); or a sympathetic friend. Bad choices are teenage boys (too distracted) and small children (not aware or coordinated enough).

At the pet shop or breeder's you will be given, or obliged to buy, a travel container. This is usually a small plastic container with holes in the lid. A roomy shoebox will suffice for a short trip, again, with holes in the lid and some bedding and a toy in it. Change and motion can be stressful for small animals, and you want to make it as easy as possible for your ham to adjust.

Avoid picking up your new pet on a day with extreme temperatures. Hamsters are susceptible to heat and cold, and abrupt shifts are also unhealthy for them. If you are a city dweller and plan to walk home with your hamster, this precaution is even more important.

If you're bringing the hamster home in a car, try to create an atmosphere of stability. One reason for bringing a companion is that this person can sit with the ham (who is in her traveling container) on his lap, steadying and talking to her. If you are on your own, the safest place to put the hamster (still in her box!) is on the floor of the passenger side of the car, unless you have really powerful heating vents there. There are no standard safety belts for hamsters, and

it takes only one jolting brake shift to shoot your pet off the seat.

Thinking like a Boy Scout

Just in case you're unlucky on the day you're bringing your hamster home and you get a flat tire, be sure that you've put plenty of bedding in the travel box (in case it's cold), have a light cloth to cover the box (in case there's glaring sun), and have a filled water bottle at the ready.

Mi Casa, Su Casa: Welcoming Hamster Home

The analogy of bringing home a newborn is not far off. Everyone in your household will want to crowd around to meet the new arrival, but what she needs is to be located as soon as possible in her new home. If you haven't bought and set up her habitat in advance, put her as quickly as possible in her safe temporary abode and keep her isolated and quiet.

After you have everything set up in the optimal spot you have chosen for her, move the temporary container over to the cage, lift her gently out (see Chapter 6 for tips on holding your hamster), and talk to her while placing her through the door or in from the top of the cage. Don't be surprised if she seems nervous or shy — wouldn't you be with large faces looming over you, in a new place that doesn't sound or smell like anywhere you know?

When you transfer your hamster to her permanent home, transfer some of the bedding she's been using as well. It will already have her scent and will reduce the trauma of being shifted around twice in one day.

For the first day or so, leave her alone, except for changing her food and water, so she has a change to settle in, make a burrow, and feel at home. Even before you go to touch her, be sure to talk to her every day, and say her name. As with many mammals, the court is still out on how much hamsters actually understand vocal patterns (no, she's never going to fetch), but hamsters do orient themselves by sound and smell. A gentle stream of conversation while she's getting used to you and your scent will help her feel that this is her family.

After a couple of days, you can begin to hold your hamster for brief periods to help her bond to you and become more socialized. But wait at least a month before letting her loose. Until she feels comfortable in her new home, she will view any freedom as a chance to escape this strange new place.

Chapter 5

Noshes, Nibbles, and Nuzzles: Caring for Your Hamster

. . . .

In This Chapter

▶ Feeding your hamster nutritiously

▶ Making hamster snacks at home

▶ Keeping hammy hydrated

▶ Setting up a hamster home gym

▶ Bringing an escapee home

. . . .

*A*fter you've created a happy home for your hamster, you want to maintain her in style, which means providing her with a healthy and varied diet and understanding her other physical needs. This chapter helps you prepare for your role as nurturer.

Filling Those Pouches: Nutrition and Feeding

Like the toys you give your hamster to keep her fit and alleviate boredom, the food you choose is designed to replicate what she eats in the wild (but with her domestic life in mind). Breeders and pet food manufacturers have been able to benefit from hamsters' long history as lab animals, through which they've learned a good deal about how hamsters eat and what they need to balance nutrition with taste. As a result, a variety of nutritionally well-balanced and tasty commercial feeds are on the market, which come in two basic types: seed mixes and extruded pellets. Depending on what's readily available at your local pet or feed store, offering a combination of feeds is best, garnished with fresh treats from your own larder.

Feeds are sold in standard 2- and 4-pound bags, or sometimes loose in bins. Don't be tempted to buy in larger quantities (if available) or store up on a bargain price, because feeds lose their nutrients if they're stored too long. (In addition to the basic ingredients, commercial feeds are fortified with essential vitamins and minerals.)

A hamster needs about a tablespoon of commercial feed a day. Because hamsters don't tend to overeat, and because they don't eat meals in one sitting, you can keep a dish partially filled and top it with treats (which I discuss momentarily) once a day. Most hamsters need 12 to 15 percent protein and 3 to 6 percent fat (check your feed package), but nursing mothers need more protein.

Aladdin's cave: Seed mixes

Seed mixes, which can be seen in most cages in pet shops, are colorful and various, with a long list of ingredients that would put a spa kitchen to shame. If you frequent health food shops, the list will probably remind you of your own breakfast (or trail mix!). Here's a typical ingredients list:

- ✔ Corn
- ✔ Dehydrated carrots
- ✔ Folic acid
- ✔ Millet
- ✔ Oat groats
- ✔ Pinto beans
- ✔ Raisins
- ✔ Split peas
- ✔ Sunflower, pumpkin, and apple seeds
- ✔ Vitamins A and E
- ✔ Wheat
- ✔ Wheat byproducts

Seed mixtures offer variety and good flavors, and they give the hamster the opportunity to forage and select her food as she might do in the wild. However, offering her this selection can prove problematic. Just as we tend to drift towards the chocolate chip cookies when we know we ought to choose the low-fat cottage cheese, hamsters sometimes eat only what appeals, thereby missing the nutritional balance that was intended by the manufacturer.

"Little boxes": Extruded cubes and pellets

There is no question that seed mixes, with their familiar ingredients, are more appealing to humans than extruded cubes and pellets. If seed mixes look like something you'd expect to be served for breakfast at a spa, extruded pellets (which resemble cigarillos) or cubes look like something NASA would dish up during your space walk. They often have some of the same combinations of fruits, vegetables, and grains that seed mixes have, but they're ground up, compressed, and chopped into regimented shapes.

While cubes and pellets aren't nearly as much fun for your hamster as seed mixes, they do guarantee that she gets all the nutrients she needs. They also have the added benefit of encouraging gnawing, which is important to keep hamsters' teeth properly worn down.

Every shape and flavor: Commercial supplements and treats

Supplements and treats function in the hamster universe much as they do in our own, as safeguards and pleasures. Vitamin and mineral supplements (A and E are especially important to hamsters) come in liquid and solid forms and are intended to add that extra guarantee that your hamster is getting all she needs in the way of nutrition, in case she's a picky eater. You can add a small dose of supplement to water or food on a daily basis.

The most common mineral supplement is the salt block or wheel, which can be placed in the food dish or hung from the side of the cage. Sometimes these supplements are fortified with other beneficial minerals, such as zinc, copper, and iodine. I have to say that my pets don't care for the salt block, but there's no accounting for taste, which is why cricket-flavored calcium tabs are also popular. (Be sure your pet supplies are kept in a separate area from your family's food!)

Treats are also packaged to look scrumptious and healthy (to us, at least). Racks and racks of brightly colored packages contain such tempting offerings as seed bars (a sort of solid version of the seed mix); dried fruits, flowers, and vegetables, such as bananas, apples, rose hips, carrots, and sweet potatoes; and seeds and nuts. Crunchy treats include sesame-coated peanut balls; yogurt chips; alfalfa "cookies"; and hamster versions of ice cream cones, Fruit Loops, and Life Savers — all made of condensed grains, fruits, and vegetables. Wooden chew sticks are also part of this group, and they come plain, colored, and in as many shapes and sizes as refrigerator magnets.

Many commercial treats use fattening corn syrup or molasses as a bonding agent, and excess sugar is no better for your hamster than it is for you, so beware of overfeeding these items.

Yogurt, mealworms, and rice — yum!

Hamsters owe their survival in the wild to their tremendous adaptability, as many a farmer has learned to his cost. Translated into domestic life, this means that hamsters are delighted to help you with your leftovers, and they also appreciate it when you throw in some hamster delicacies (see Figure 5-1). Here's a partial list of favorites, but feel free to offer other taste treats:

- Apples
- Bananas
- Bread
- Broccoli
- Carrots
- Cauliflower
- Celery
- Corn
- Cottage cheese
- Eggs (hard boiled or scrambled)
- Grapes
- Lettuce
- Pasta
- Peanuts

  ✔ Raisins

  ✔ Rice (boiled)

  ✔ Strawberries

  ✔ Tomatoes

  ✔ Yogurt

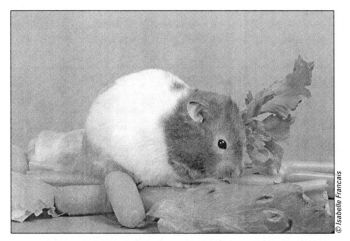

Figure 5-1: Hamsters enjoy fresh veggie treats.

Two items you're probably not going to find in your own cupboards, but that hamsters regard as particularly delectable, are crickets and mealworms. These are readily available at pet stores, if you can bear to handle them. (Don't worry about dispatching them — your hamster will take care of that!)

Hamsters like new taste sensations, so supplement a good commercial feed with a selection of fresh treats. Cut them into manageable chunks, but don't mince or process them — chewing is good for your hamster. Be sure to rinse fresh foods.

Hay, you!

All herbivores need roughage, so in addition to the Technicolor feeds and snacks you provide, you should supply a small pile of hay each day. Timothy and alfalfa are the most common (they have the highest levels of nutrients), although I've also seen an oat/wheat/barley mix. Common sized packages are 5 ounce, 1 pound, and 1 pound 4 ounce, but if you live in horse or cow country you may be able to negotiate for some of your neighbors' leftover hay.

How Hamsters Eat

Domesticated animals retain behaviors that helped them survive in the wild, and hamsters are no exception. They are programmed to put something away for a rainy day, and a hamster often fills her pouches with the food you put down, to be emptied into her nest later (see Figure 5-2). For this reason, you want to feed raw, fresh, and unprocessed cooked foods sparingly so hoarded food won't spoil. Also, be sure to clean away all scattered or buried food when you clear out the bedding once a week (see Chapter 4).

Figure 5-2: A hamster stores food in her cheek pouches.

A hamster can stuff her cheeks fuller than the size of her own head, and with a quantity of food that equals her own body weight!

What not to feed

Rodent gourmands they may be, but even a hamster's metabolism has trouble digesting some foods. Here are some things not to put on the menu:

✓ Unripe fruits or vegetables

✓ Canned fruits or vegetables

✓ Leafy greens in excess — kale, spinach, romaine, and other dark greens, which can cause diarrhea

Sons of the Desert Need Water Too

Fresh water is an important part of your hamster's diet, helping to cleanse the system, facilitate digestion, and prevent dehydration. Your pet will drink at his own pace, so be sure to check and refill the water bottle constantly. Filtered water is better if you can afford it.

Keep an eye out for residue inside the bottle — after a while the sides will get cloudy with mineral buildup, which makes the water brackish. When this happens it's time to get a new bottle, because these are too small to scrub effectively inside.

Heart Like a Wheel

You don't have to have children to get the point of educational toys or a personal trainer to understand the importance of fitness. Likewise, you don't have to be a hamster to grasp why exercise and stimulation are important to your diminutive, but dynamic, pet. Hams can run up to 8 miles a day using their powerful forelegs — another legacy from their desert life, when they often traveled miles in search of food or a new domain. That's why, as I discuss in Chapter 4, an exercise wheel in the cage is a must (see Figure 5-3).

Some researchers think that excessive running is a sign of anxiety or boredom (not to mention a sign that you'll be driven crazy), so be sure your hamster has other recreational options, too. Chapter 4 offers lots of suggestions.

Figure 5-3: An exercise wheel is a necessary accessory.

Bad Hair Days: Grooming Your Hamster

Actually, a bad hair day for a hamster is a sign of poor health. These fastidious pets groom themselves constantly, as fussy as Lewis Carroll's White Rabbit exclaiming over his paws and whiskers. In the wild, cleanliness removes your scent from predators, while spreading it around among friends and family. (Who needs a long-distance phone plan when you have ears, nose, and whiskers to tell you all the news?)

However, deep bedding does sometimes cling to a hamster's tousled fur, especially in the long-haired varieties, and she may be happy to have you help get her coat in order. You can do this gently with your fingers, a soft toothbrush, or a doll's hairbrush or comb (see Figure 5-4).

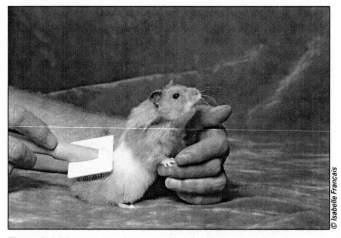

© Isabelle Francais

Figure 5-4: You may need to occasionally groom your hamster.

Unless your hamster has escaped and gotten into something gooey, viscous, or toxic, you don't need to bathe him. In fact, doing so risks causing him to catch cold.

Hamster on the Loose

In Chapter 4, I explain how to create a safe haven so your hamster can come out for a visit, but that doesn't mean your resident Houdini won't make an unauthorized escape attempt. If this happens, clear the room of avid pets, panicky children, and bossy "helpers." Set up a trail of treats leading to an enclosed space like a box or bucket (not a closet), and be patient. You may think of your hamster as "escaped," but he may think he has just gone foraging, and he'll be perfectly ready to return to his burrow soon.

The time you've spent getting to know your hamster is amply repaid in this situation. You know whether he prefers peanuts or grapes as an enticement, and he knows how you smell. Actually, you want to avoid feeling panicked precisely because your fear will be communicated to your hamster through your scent, and it will make him fearful as well.

Don't worry if your ploys don't pay off immediately. Just when you've given up hope, you'll look across the room and your hamster will be sitting up on his haunches, waiting for dinner. See if he takes the bait, or try to approach slowly, while talking to him, with a lidless container like a large cup or coffee tin to put over him quickly. Do not run or lunge, which will terrify your hamster, who is much faster than you are. And do not grab — in your anxiety, you can easily hurt these fragile animals.

Chapter 6

Baby, What's Your Sign? Getting to Know Your Hamster

In This Chapter

▶ Reading your hamster's body language

▶ Dealing with fighting hamsters

▶ Holding your hamster

▶ Identifying your hamster's gender

*Y*ou've found the hamster of your dreams, set her up in style, figured out what her favorite dishes are, and worked out an exercise regime, but something's missing — you never talk. What's she saying to you when she squeaks, twitches her nose, or raises her paws? If you have brought home two or more hamsters, what are they saying to each other? How do you know when their relationship is going wrong, or when it's going so right that you may end up with a few extra hams on your hands? Fear not: Answers await in this chapter.

A Twitch is Worth a Thousand Words

Hamsters take in information about the world through their noses, ears, whiskers, and eyes, and much of their body language is designed to facilitate these fact-gathering techniques. They then respond to perceived pleasures or threats. For example, if two or more hamsters are together, they sniff and circle each other to determine sex and dominance, and then they decide if they wish to relax, entice, or fight! Table 6-1 lists some common hamster postures and what they mean.

Table 6-1	Hamster Postures
Physical Signs	*Translation*
Erect ears, twitching nose and whiskers	Curious but not alarmed
Ears tilted forward, cheeks puffed out, teeth bared	Angry, frightened, or both
Grooming and stretching	Confident and relaxed. (However, constant, obsessive grooming is a sign of anxiety.)
Ears back, posture tense	Dread and defense
Erect on hind legs, feinting motions	Aggressive; an "I could have been a contender" stance
Cowering	Fearful; "Oh dear, I know something awful's out there."

The behaviors listed in this table are typical responses to stimuli. However, each hamster is unique, anid you'll soon discover how to distinguish your hamster's subtle gestures: a curious cock of the head, a cheerful scramble in the bedding for a toy or treat, or an imperious squeak that says, "Where's my 4 o'clock raisin?"

Boys Will Be Boys

Don't say I didn't warn you: Mature male hamsters, especially the more solitary Syrians, fight for dominance if they are kept together. (Female Syrians are also combative.) And unfortunately, in the relatively confined spaces of a typical cage, they may need to resolve this tricky social issue more than once. You've probably seen enough nature films to recognize the signs: The dominant male walks stiffly and intimidatingly, sometimes actually trying to flip his opponent, while the submissive male sometimes holds out an appeasing paw or rolls over. If they can't work things out through this posturing, a lot of running, rolling, and biting ensues, which can get dangerous (not to mention noisy).

Fighting hamsters are much like fighting dogs: If you get in the middle of a scrap, you're fair game and are likely to be scratched or bitten yourself. (It's a boy thing.) If you need to break up a fight, first try spritzing the combatants with water to startle them; then go in with gloves on and a container of some kind to remove the underdog.

Gotta burrow

The way to offer your hamster the best of all possible worlds is to allow him to create an environment that feels instinctively natural while affording him all the amusements of domestic life. (See Chapter 4 for ideas.) Burrowing is a way of keeping house for hamsters, just as they used to in the desert and steppes of the wild. A hamster snuggled deep into his bedding, or digging a cache, is a hamster who feels that all's right with his world.

Hamster Uglies: Dealing with Problem Behavior

Except for natural fighting among males (and sometimes among hamsters who haven't been raised together), maladjustment is rare in hamsters. Occasionally, a fearful hamster will bite — this is almost always a defensive mechanism in a prey species.

If your hamster is fearful or aggressive on a regular basis (keep in mind that anyone can have a bad day), try to remove any stressors, such as loud music or another hamster sharing his quarters. Then work to gently socialize this traumatized animal. Most nervous animals respond to what behavioralists call *desensitization*: the act of pairing a negative event (such as being held or moved) with positive reinforcement (like a treat or stroking) until the event loses its negative connotations. If your hamster seems really frightened when you hold her, start slowly by holding out an enticing bit of fruit or seed, and soon she'll be standing up looking for you.

A Handful of Hamster

To make handling your hamster a pleasant and safe experience for both of you, you must know how to hold her correctly. And it helps to understand her point of view. You've probably seen at least one monster movie where a giant gorilla, lizard, or ogre carries the helpless heroine away. Perhaps you've always identified with the girl, but to a hamster, you're the monster!

Ham-stars

All hamsters are entertaining, but some have actually become part of the entertainment industry!

Mystery novelist Janet Evanovich is the author of nine novels featuring spunky Jersey girl turned bounty hunter Stephanie Plum. Stephanie has two very attractive men vying for her affections, but her best friend is her hamster, Rex, whom she describes as the "small, silent type."

The British animated comic spy series *Danger Mouse* featured the jaunty hero's gloomy companion, a hamster named Penfold.

Hamsters have become real favorites in Japanese anime, including such adventures as Ebichu the Housekeeping Hamster and the Cartoon Network's Hamtaro.

Holding on

Pick up your hamster so he feels safe and you have sufficient control over sudden pops or escape attempts. Here are some holds to try:

- ✓ **The scoop:** Gently lift your hamster by his rear end. Hold him as you would a baby, with one hand cupping his middle, or just under his front legs, and the other supporting his bottom (see Figure 6-1).

- ✓ **The cuddle:** This is a variation on the scoop, with the hamster held firmly against your chest.

- ✓ **The dish:** After you've lifted him from the cage or enclosure, hold him in your cupped hands as if he were lying in the bottom of a shallow dish. This hold is risky with some of the smaller, more hectic hamsters, like Dwarf Russians, who tend to bounce right out!

- ✓ **The nape hold:** Grasp the hamster firmly by the loose skin at the back of his neck (see Figure 6-2). This hold usually has the effect of partially opening his mouth and, as you may imagine, is not a universal favorite among hamsters. However, this maneuver is useful if you need to check his teeth, examine him for injuries, administer medication, or stop a fight.

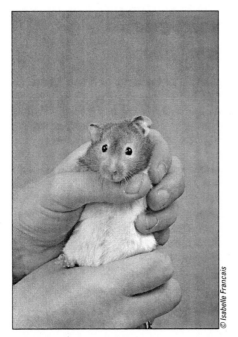

Figure 6-1: The scoop hold.

Figure 6-2: The nape hold.

Teaching children to handle a hamster

In Chapter 2, I discuss the importance of ensuring that your children are old enough to have a responsible relationship with a pet. But even children old enough to take on the responsibility may be young enough to have coordination and attention span issues that compromise their ability to safely hold a hamster.

Make sure your children understand that a hamster's life depends on how carefully she's held. Use a simile that your children can relate to: The hamster is a precious doll, a precious plate, or just like a baby sister. Encourage your children to hold the hamster only over a surface, such as a table or sofa, to minimize risks. Make your children feel important and responsible, and chances are they will behave importantly and responsibly.

Sex and the Single Hamster

Hamster gender isn't distinguished by bold coloration, plumage, muscle mass, or fashion sense, but boys and girls are still fairly easy to tell apart. (Hamsters do this by checking out each other's scent glands, but that's not a language we speak, so we need visual clues.) You need to hold your hamster firmly upright (probably by using the nape hold I describe in the previous section). Here's what to look for:

- ✓ **Girls:** The genital area and the anus, which look like two lines or dashes, are very close together — about ¼ inch apart. Female hamsters also have teats (usually seven pairs), but these are not always visible on the long-haired breeds.

- ✓ **Boys:** The genital area and anus are farther apart, perhaps as much as ½ inch. On more mature males, both the penile area and testes may be visible, while the whole nether region is a little fleshier.

Responsible pet stores segregate hamsters by sex and train their staff members to tell the difference, but you don't want to take any chances. Before you buy, make sure that you and a staff member check the sex of all the hamsters in a given enclosure. If the sexes are mixed, realize that you are taking a calculated risk by purchasing a female, who may already be impregnated.

Chapter 7

In the Pink: Hamster Health and Breeding Issues

*D*ealing with health issues is a critical part of caring for any pet. A hamster's small body and rapid metabolism mean that sickness and injury can have severe consequences if not identified and dealt with quickly.

In this chapter, I make you aware of common hamster health problems and how to address them. I also briefly discuss responsible breeding, helping you to decide if you really want to double, triple, or quadruple your hamster pleasure — and responsibility.

The Healthy Hamster

In Chapter 3, I talk about how to find a healthy hamster to become your pet. A healthy hamster:

✔ Has bright eyes
✔ Is alert and inquisitive
✔ Has healthy skin and coat
✔ Has well-formed teeth
✔ Is shapely and plump
✔ Dozes during the day and is active at night
✔ Moves freely and playfully, but not compulsively

Now that we're talking about the health of *your* hamster, you need to add your knowledge of your own pet's appearance and habits to this list of the basic signs of health. If you notice a significant change in how your hamster looks or behaves, you need to determine if that change is being caused by an illness or injury.

Sneezes, Wheezes, and Other Hamster Health Problems

Hamsters, like most mammals, are prone to colds and respiratory disorders, digestive complaints, and skin problems, as well as injuries like cuts and bruises. If you suspect your hamster is sick:

- ✔ Separate him from other hamsters.

- ✔ Hold him gently and examine him.

- ✔ Change his food, bedding, and water.

- ✔ Wash all toys and exercise equipment.

- ✔ Wash your own hands thoroughly after handling your hamster because bacteria are transmittable.

If your ham has a minor ailment, such as a cold, you can try to heal her at home. However, you need to call the vet at the first sign of any acute symptoms, such as the following:

- ✔ Labored breathing

- ✔ Rigid posture

- ✔ A serious wound or abscess

- ✔ Tumors (see the "Lumps and bumps" section later in the chapter)

- ✔ Signs of parasites or fungal infection (see the "Skin ailments" section later in the chapter)

- ✔ Any symptom of wet tail or severe gastric distress (see the "Wet tail" section later in the chapter)

Many hamster ailments, including potentially fatal wet tail, are brought on, or intensified, by stress. Use the tips I provide in Chapters 2 and 4 to create a safe, stress-free environment for your pet.

Colds

Hamsters are sensitive to temperature and can catch cold easily in damp or drafty environments. Symptoms include lethargy, loss of appetite, and a runny nose and/or eye — in other words, just what you'd see in a toddler or yourself. Your response to a cold should be to move the hamster away from any drafts, provide lots of deep bedding and a sunlamp, and monitor him to see if the condition worsens, which may require antibiotics from the vet.

Because they rely on benign bacteria, many antibiotics are fatal to hamsters, including penicillin, ampicillin, erythromycin, lincomycin, and vancomycin. Don't take chances: Be sure your vet knows this.

Diabetes

While less common in hamsters than it used to be (because of more careful breeding practices), diabetes still crops up, most often in Dwarf Campbell's hamsters and some crossbreeds. Symptoms include excessive drinking and urinating, trembling, and, in extreme cases, coma. Your response should be to immediately seek veterinary care, but don't expect miracles. Treatments have advanced in recent years, but it's hard to regulate the glucose level of a very small animal. If your ham is diagnosed with diabetes, feed him only fresh foods, as almost all commercial feeds contain some kind of sugar.

Eye infections

Hams are prone to eye infections. The symptoms are gummy, runny eyes or discharge. Your response should be to clean the affected area with soft gauze (not cotton balls, which shred) and call the vet, who may prescribe eyedrops.

Heat stroke/dehydration

Hamsters are just as sensitive to high temperatures as they are to low ones. On a warm day, or in a stuffy room or car, your ham may start panting and behaving sluggishly, which are signs of heat stroke. Your response should be to gently wipe your pet down with cool water until his breathing normalizes, get him out of the heat, give him access to water, and get him to the vet quickly so he can have his electrolytes replenished.

Dehydration is usually a symptom of some other disorder, such as kidney failure or diabetes. Symptoms of dehydration include excessive thirst, dull coat, and weight loss. Your response should be to get your pet to the vet as soon as possible.

Lumps and bumps

Active lives and small bodies sometimes make for small nicks, which can easily be missed (see the "Wounds" section later in the chapter). If a cut or skin puncture gets infected and heals over, an *abscess* — a painful hard or puffy area — is likely to form. The symptoms include redness, swelling, pain, and loss of appetite. Your vet needs to drain the abscess with a needle and put the patient on some antibiotics.

Tumors and cysts, which are sometimes indicative of cancer and sometimes benign, may distort the surface of the body if they're external and can often be surgically removed. Be aware that if your pet is diagnosed with cancer, there is a limit to how much intervention is possible and practical.

Obsessive/compulsive behavior

Human beings have not cornered the market in anxiety disorders. For hamsters, pacing and compulsive backflipping are inherited genetic disorders for which there is no cure. But before you assume you have the Norman Bates of hamsters in your cage, check for possible stressors — loud music, children, bright lights — because many hamsters develop compulsive patterns when they are not happy campers. For clinical compulsion, euthanasia is suggested, because the hamster is leading an exhausting life beyond its control.

Respiratory problems

Breathing difficulties in hamsters are sometimes a sign of acute problems, such as heart failure or severe intestinal disorders. However, other than heat stroke, the most common reason for wheezing is allergies.

Hamsters are very sensitive to dust, to additives in bedding (see Chapter 4 for a warning about using cedar shavings), to industrial cleansers, and even to perfume. They can also have allergic reactions to foods. If your ham is breathing abnormally and you've ruled out excessive heat as the cause, here are some steps you can take:

- ✔ Replace his bedding with anything natural and dust free (such as shredded paper or old towels) until you can get to the pet shop to find an alternative product.

- ✔ If you think there may be cleanser residue in his area, move the cage and wipe the space down with warm water.

- ✔ Be sure the culprit isn't you (such as your aftershave or perfume).

- ✔ Review your pet's diet with your vet when you take him in.

Skin ailments

Hamsters are susceptible to parasites, especially mites, and to fungal invasions like ringworm. The symptoms include scaly skin, scratching, and hair loss. (Keep in mind that red, scaly skin is also sometimes indicative of an allergic reaction.) Your response should be to see your vet because both conditions require a course of medication. Be especially careful to wash your hands after handling your hamster — these nasties are transmittable to other pets and humans.

Tummy troubles

Hamsters can have rich and varied diets (see Chapter 5), and they can sometimes suffer from diarrhea or constipation. The causes are often the same as in humans: not enough roughage, too much roughage, too many rich fruits or vegetables, or a sudden change in diet. A ham with constipation will arch her back and strain to defecate. A ham with diarrhea will have loose stool and general uncleanliness. Mild cases of either condition are usually cured by a change in diet: More green vegetables and a little olive oil in an eye dropper help constipation, and a decrease in green vegetables and increase in roughage help with mild diarrhea.

Sometimes digestive troubles, especially acute diarrhea, signal more serious complications, such as wet tail or parasite infection. Acute diarrhea drains a hamster's tiny body of vital nutrients. If your pet doesn't come around within a day, get him to the vet quickly!

Wet tail

This severe, and often fatal, bacterial sickness manifests itself as acute diarrhea — hence the name. The afflicted hamster is sluggish, won't eat or drink, is nervous and agitated, and has ruffled, unkempt fur — a real sign of distress in this tidy animal. Rectal bleeding or *prolapse* (where the rectum protrudes because of damage to the colon and intestines) is also common. This disease often affects young and/or transplanted hamsters and is thought to be stress related. If your hamster has diarrhea for more than a day, get her to the vet immediately.

Wounds

Adult hamsters may fight, or play fight, so cuts and bruises from fellow hamsters are a possibility. And damaged toys or exercise equipment are another source of these types of injuries. Unless the wound is fresh and bleeding, you may have a hard time detecting it, which is why you should check your hamster over thoroughly each time you hold him. If you see a minor wound, wash it gently with soap or diluted hydrogen peroxide. Do not use ointments, which mat the coat into the wound and prevent healing. (Your hamster will probably lick them off anyway.)

Poor appetite or swollen pouches may indicate a wound from mis-aligned teeth. (See Chapter 3 for details about healthy teeth.)

Aging Gracefully

Because hams have a relatively short lifespan (see Chapter 2), you may begin to see some signs of aging in their second year. These signs include:

- ✓ Hair loss
- ✓ Thinning of the body
- ✓ Reduced activity

As long as your hamster has a normal appetite and is still playful and happy to see you, you have no reason to be concerned. You can tell hair loss that is the result of aging because it's not accompanied by the scaly, red skin that allergies, fungi, or parasites induce.

Goodnight, Sweet Hamlet

Whether because of old age or an untreatable condition, at some point you'll need to say goodbye to your friend. Many rodents die quietly in their sleep. However, if you face the difficult decision of euthanasia, your vet — who should be someone you trust — will tell you when that choice makes sense.

If you have some advance warning that your pet is very ill, create a ritual that allows you — and especially your children — to say goodbye. Don't feel silly: This small creature has been a member of your family.

Many vets offer inexpensive cremation, if you'd like to scatter your pet's ashes or if you live in an area where pet burial is difficult or not permitted.

Becoming a Hamster Grandparent

Deciding to breed your hamster is as serious a decision as deciding to bring any other life into the world. Do not make the decision lightly, and be sure that you and the rest of your family are ready for all the chores, as well as the pleasures.

Here's an ugly fact: Five million homeless animals are destroyed in the United States each year. Do not add irresponsibly to the surplus population. Do not breed hamsters just because you think babies are cute or that your kids will have fun. (Trust me: They'll be thrilled until the pull of Nintendo or the Powerpuff Girls or field hockey gets too strong.) And don't assume that breeding is a road to riches: It isn't.

Plan carefully; read everything you can find about safe, successful breeding; and find homes for your pups in advance if you don't intend to keep or show your hamsters. Are we clear? Good, now you're ready to become a grandparent to the fourth power!

Bring her some ice cream — and a cricket!

A female hamster over the age of 3 to 4 weeks comes into season every 4 days for about 12 hours, usually at night. (However, she shouldn't be bred until she is about 4 months old.) Her body language (lowered back, splayed legs) tells you when, and this is the time to introduce Mr. Right for an overnight stay. If you misread the signs, she'll let you know! After these two have mated, you may see a whitish deposit in the vaginal area, and your Juliet will want nothing more to do with Romeo.

Homes for your hamsters

Need hamster godparents?

- ✔ Place an enticing ad in the "Pets" section of your local paper — with baby pics!
- ✔ Post notices on bulletin boards at pet and feed stores and at the vet's.
- ✔ Talk to your local school.
- ✔ Make deals with your friends — two boxes of Girl Scout cookies for one hamster.

Be sure that you check with professional breeders, and on the Web sites listed in the back of this book, for advice on genetically safe breeding combinations. Some hamster strains cannot be combined without risking behavioral or birth defects.

If you think human moms-to-be can get cranky, just wait. Pregnant hamsters can be aggressive, eat and drink more (of course), and often burrow constantly (becoming Susie Homemakers). Gestation takes between 15 and 18 days for Syrians and between 18 and 22 days for Campbell's, Chinese, Robovorski, and Winter White hams. And youth is fleeting: Females over a year old generally can't have babies.

The miracle of birth

An average litter consists of between 5 and 15 pups, born sequentially. Unless the mom-to-be is having an obvious problem, your job is to stay out of the way. (Just be sure you've provided plenty of food and water.)

Like many animals, hamsters often give birth at night, when they feel safest, so the only indication you may have is that your hamster disappears into her nest. Do nothing. Although the actual birthing takes only 10 to 30 minutes, she needs privacy for about a week; hamster moms who feel threatened eat their young. (They sometimes eat babies anyway, if they think there are too many or sense that some are weak; this is nature taking its course, and interfering only makes things worse.) Do not attempt to handle pups for at least two weeks; then you can gently shift the babies so you can clean the cage. At about three weeks, you can begin to tame them.

Family life

Hamster newborns look like boiled peanuts and are pretty helpless (see Figure 7-1). By 14 to 18 days, their eyes are beginning to open and their fur is growing in, and after 3 weeks to a month you should be looking to separate them if they're Syrians or, in the case of other breeds, separate the boys from the girls. Young hamsters also begin to play and to make their own nests and territories, so be sure you've got a cage that gives them plenty of personal space.

Step back and admire the lovely golden, tortoiseshell, gray, or banded coats of this newest generation of hamsters, and consider that you and they are part of history, each descending from that first, fateful desert encounter between hamster and man — a 300-year journey from the ancient East to your home. ("Yeah, yeah," your hamster says, "May I please have a treat now?")

© Lorraine Hill, Acorn Stock Images

Figure 7-1: A litter of hams.

The Hams Are Out There: Ten Interesting Hamster Web Sites

A note of caution: Enthusiast sites are sometimes short-lived. These Web addresses are functioning as of this book's publication.

- ✔ www.hamsterland.com
  This well-organized site for hamster aficionados features good links and major marketing partners, which suggests it has staying power.

- ✔ www.hamsterhideout.com
  This charming site has a hamster forum, fun links, and delightful photos.

- ✔ www.hamsterific.com
  A site for informal hobbyists, it features tips on common household problems.

- ✔ www.hamsterama.co.uk
  Managed by two English breeders, this site has some nice links, photos, and a useful FAQs section.

- ✔ www.hamsters.co.uk
  This site is actually the hamster section of a major pet product site, www.petwebsite.com, and is oriented towards gifts and hamster-related products. Although the site is based in the United Kingdom, the product links are international.

- ✔ www.petwebsite.com
  This home page for the previous site has useful links to general pet resources and other rodent information.

- ✔ www.angelfire.com/id/jacheong/hamster.html
  This lively site has links to other hobbyists and very amusing animated graphics.

- ✔ www.hamtaro.com
  Hamtaro is a Japanese anime series, now on the Cartoon Network, starring a pet hamster who shares adventures with his fifth-grade owner, Laura.

- ✔ www.hamstertours.com
  For hamster owners with a sense of humor, this site includes fantasy hamster products, poetry, and unusual links.

- ✔ http://groups.msn.com/hamstersgalore
  This URL takes you to the MSN chat room called Hamsters Galore.

Condensed Hamsters: Ten Common Questions

✔ **Are hamsters clean?**
Yes, they have no natural odor and are fastidious groomers.

✔ **Are they good with children?**
For a child 10 or older, a hamster is the perfect introduction to pet love and responsibility.

✔ **Are they safe to handle?**
Unless sick or frightened, hamsters rarely bite; your biggest problem is that they may jump out of your hands.

✔ **Is it safe to buy one from a pet store?**
Yes, responsible pet stores and chains sell healthy pets that are well cared for. Just be sure that you like the look of the place and the staff is attentive and knowledgeable.

✔ **How long do hamsters live?**
The average lifespan is between two and three years, but they pack a lot of living into a short time!

✔ **Should I get a boy or a girl?**
Hamsters of either sex behave pretty much the same, but be sure not to get a boy *and* a girl, unless you want lots of hamsters.

✔ **Should I get more than one so they have company?**
Syrian, Chinese, and Roborovski hamsters prefer to live alone; Winter White (Dwarf Russian) hamsters and Campbell's hamsters can live together, but they don't need to.

✔ **Can I play with my hamster?**
Actually, you'll have more fun watching your hamster play with her toys herself.

✔ **What's with the wheel?**
Hamsters need constant exercise to stay healthy and happy. Think what a good example they set!

✔ **How do I show my hamster?**
Check out some of the Web links in the list on the previous page, and contact the most established American breed club, the California Hamster Association (calhamassoc@ hotmail.com), or the Internet Hamster Association (http:// groups.msn.com/InternetHamsterAssociation/home/ msnw).

Index

FOR DUMMIES

Pet care essentials in plain English

DOG BREEDS

Boxers For Dummies
0-7645-5285-6

German Shepherds For Dummies
0-7645-5280-5

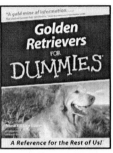

Golden Retrievers For Dummies
0-7645-5267-8

Labrador Retrievers For Dummies
0-7645-5281-3

Pugs For Dummies
0-7645-54076-9

Retired Racing Greyhounds For Dummies
0-7645-5276-7

Siberian Huskies For Dummies
0-7645-5279-1

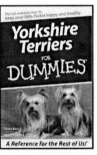

Yorkshire Terriers For Dummies
0-7645-6880-9

Also available:

Jack Russell Terriers For Dummies
(0-7645-5268-6)

Rottweilers For Dummies
(0-7645-5271-6)

Chihuahuas For Dummies
(0-7645-5284-8)

Dachshunds For Dummies
(0-7645-5289-9)

Pit Bulls For Dummies
(0-7645-5291-0)

DOG CARE, HEALTH, TRAINING, & BEHAVIOR

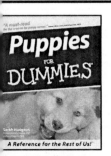

Puppies For Dummies
0-7645-5255-4

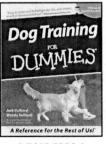

Dog Training For Dummies
0-7645-5286-4

Senior Dogs For Dummies
0-7645-5818-8

Also available:

Choosing a Dog For Dummies
(0-7645-5310-0)

Dog Health & Nutrition For Dummies
(0-7645-5318-6)

Dog Tricks For Dummies
(0-7645-5287-2)

House Training For Dummies
(0-7645-5349-6)

Dogs For Dummies, 2nd Edition
(0-7645-5274-0)

FOR DUMMIES®

Pet care essentials in plain English

CATS & KITTENS

0-7645-5275-9

0-7645-4150-1

BIRDS

0-7645-5139-6

0-7645-5311-9

AMPHIBIANS & REPTILES

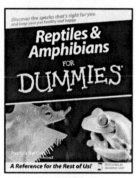

0-7645-2569-7

0-7645-5313-5

0-7645-5260-0

FISH & AQUARIUMS

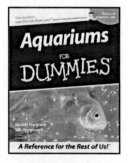

0-7645-5156-6

0-7645-5340-2

SMALL ANIMALS

0-7645-5259-7

0-7645-0861-X

CPSIA information can be obtained at www.ICGtesting.com
Printed in the USA
BVOW02n1609280614

357244BV00006B/1/P